Our Relational God

Our Relational God

Danny Kershen

RESOURCE *Publications* • Eugene, Oregon

OUR RELATIONAL GOD

Resource Publications
An Imprint of Wipf and Stock Publishers
199 W. 8th Ave., Suite 3
Eugene, OR 97401

www.wipfandstock.com

PAPERBACK ISBN: 978-1-7252-9076-1
HARDCOVER ISBN: 978-1-7252-9077-8
EBOOK ISBN: 978-1-7252-9078-5

03/04/21

To my father, Ron Kershen,
whose quiet but deep faith and Christ-like attitude
toward life and people have left an indelible mark
on those who know him, especially his middle son.

Set your minds on things above, not on earthly things.

—Colossians 3:2

"No longer will they teach their neighbor, or say to one another, 'Know the Lord,' because they will all know me, from the least of them to the greatest," declares the Lord. "For I will forgive their wickedness and will remember their sins no more."

—Jeremiah 31:34

Contents

SECTION ONE

Considering Faith

Glow-in-the-Dark God

I BELIEVE THERE ARE many people in the world who struggle with the hiddenness of God. Having experienced the blandness of everyday life, along with the tedium of continuing to put one foot in front of the other, there are those who would say God seems a million miles away, totally inaccessible, or maybe not there at all. In the grips of this mindset, it is easy to see how one could view the universe as mindless and uncaring as the same mundane cycles repeat over and over with the same unsatisfying results. A person could begin to feel more like a cog than a human. Looking for a ray of sunshine in a grey existence, it would not be strange for someone to cry out to God, "Where are you? I need something more!" I know I have.

I remember lying awake in bed late at night asking God to talk to me. I really wanted to have a conversation with him. I wanted him to speak to me about all the important things in life; console me over the difficulties I was encountering; impart wisdom like a father from the final scene of a 1950s TV show, wrapping up the lesson from that thirty-minute episode in a neat, heartwarming package. But he didn't. I now realize there were reasons why he didn't. But back then, it was frustrating, and I felt there was a great distance between me and my heavenly father. It is in those moments you tend to doubt.

I think many people have had experiences similar to mine. Your friendly neighborhood Christian will tell you religion is all about having a relationship with God. Yet, how does one relate with a God you cannot see? They say we are supposed to listen to God, but have you ever heard his voice? I've heard he wants to be with us, but I can't touch him. It is easy to see how this relationship would seem difficult or even impossible.

When I was around 12 years old, there was something exciting going on in my hometown. I grew up in the small, sleepy town of Canyon, Texas. Being in the panhandle, it wasn't very far past being a farming community. A description of Canyon would include words like flat, dry, brown, and windy. Not exactly exciting. There was rarely anything to get enthusiastic about. Its main attraction was the local college but beyond that, there was not a lot to do. That was about to change.

Out on the edge of town, a company was in the process of building a brand-new skating rink! As cool as that was, it was rumored that this rink would be different. Most rinks have a wooden floor, not unlike a basketball court. If the floor is not well maintained, you start to feel every nook and cranny under your wheels as you roll from slat to slat. But our rink was going to have a new technology called a poured floor. They used a fancy polyurethane product and literally poured it over concrete. As it settled and dried, it created a glass-smooth surface with extra grip for when you were flying around the corners at break-neck speed.

As splendid as that was, it was not the truly exciting part. You see, the floor was almost transparent. Under the poured floor, on the concrete, they had painted something that you could hardly see. When the fluorescent lights were on, it appeared a pale yellowish color. They also used this hidden paint to create designs all over the walls of the facility. Why would they waste so much time and effort painting something basically invisible to the eye? That was the special part. When the lights went low, something magical happened. The paint began to glow.

The skating rink was transformed into an entire galaxy! It had an otherworldly luminosity and the physical building faded into the background. I went from skating in little Canyon, Texas, to being surrounded by stars and planets in deep space. As the terrestrial bodies passed underneath my wheels, it was easy to imagine flying across the galaxy in a spaceship strapped to my feet.

Fittingly, the new skating rink was named the Galaxy Skateway. I spent many nights there, having fun with my friends, honing my skating skills, and enjoying the feeling of flying through the stars every time the lights went low. When the lights went up, the galaxy faded away, but having experienced it, I always knew that it was there.

I hope you are beginning to see the point of my story. It is analogous to God's hiddenness. God may seem like he is not there, but given the right circumstances, he becomes central and the entire material world fades to the background. I believe spiritual things are like this. We spend most of our time focused on the material world right in front of us, but behind this physical veil is the greater reality.

The skeptic might look at my analogy and say, "But the glow-in-the-dark galaxy you are describing is an illusion! So, God is an illusion as well." To that point, let me say two things. First, it is an analogy and no analogy is perfect. Second, the paint and the design were real. Someone created them. They were there whether the lights were on or off. They simply became much more visible under the right conditions. When we "dim" the florescent lights of the material world, there is so much to see. The Bible calls this seeing with your spiritual eyes.

I am going to spend much of this book dimming the fluorescent lights and helping you see this glow-in-the-dark God. The wonderful news is that he is not just there, he wants to relate with us. In fact, relating is central to who he is and what he is about. Connections are woven into the very fabric of his creation and, throughout the Bible, pretty much everything God does has a relational aspect. Maybe you don't believe me. Let's do a quick thought experiment to begin to explore this notion.

Try to imagine anything—anything at all. It could be an animal, vegetable, or mineral. It could be big or small. It could be material or immaterial. It doesn't matter. Got it? Good. Now, take that thing and try and think of at least one thing that it is connected to in some way. Did something pop into your head? Whatever it is, it shows it relates to something else.

This exercise can be a game you can play with someone else. Your friend comes up with something and you think of something to which it connects. Then your friend takes your connection and connects it to something else. The game can go on and on. Here is a quick example:

Everyone enjoys having fun. Fun is connected to recreation. A type of recreation is baseball. Baseball players use a glove. Gloves can also be work gloves. Work gloves are a form of protection. Protection can also be a shield. A shield often goes with a sword. A sword is sharp. A sharp person is smart. A smart person can find many more connections in God's creation.

See what I mean? As you play this game, you may find something you think does not have a connection. Congratulations. But, how hard did you have to try? Doesn't that mean that associations are far and away the norm? Also, you may not find a connectedness simply because you can't define that thing.

I had a tough time coming up with things related to a black hole. It would be easy to say it relates to space, but what is it and what purpose does it have? I realized that my lack of understanding about black holes is what makes it hard to see the connections. So, the principle appears to be, the more you know about something, the easier it is to see how it relates. It would be helpful if you kept that principle in mind as you continue through this book.

Perhaps you are still skeptical. That is fine. I am only hoping to pique your interest at this point. There is much more to discover. I invite you to read on and decide for yourself, because I really want you to meet Our Relational God.

The Evolution of Faith

God has a sense of humor. I believe this because of what he has done in my life. If you knew me, you would easily perceive that I should not be writing a book about relationality. That would be because I'm an introvert. I would rather sit alone in my living room watching the TV than to put forth the energy to interact with other people. I go long periods without reaching out to any of my friends or family. Yes, I realize that is rude and I should do better. I guess that's why they often sound surprised when I do call!

Relating for me is often more of a chore than a pleasure. It's not that I don't like people, I just prefer being by myself. Yet, God placed it on my heart to write a book about how relational he is. Funny.

But even this little joke of God's is evidence of his relationality. Doing something humorous is doing something relational. A gag is meant to be played on someone else. A joke is pointless if no one is there to laugh. Besides, how could an introvert like me come up with this book idea if it were not for God's nudging?

When we start talking about God and his relationality, we are delving into the realm of belief, or faith. If I make the statement, "God is relational," I am making some belief assumptions that should stand up to scrutiny. I am assuming that there is a God and that he has characteristics that we can learn and evaluate.

So, it would be helpful to take a few steps back and look at how one could arrive there. Let's examine the different ways people deal with the subject of God and see if relationality plays a role. I will call this journey, "the Evolution of Faith."

We are all confronted with the concept of God as we journey through life. Therefore, we all must form some type of opinion. Some people may say they have no opinion about God. But that is just holding the opinion that God is not worth looking into. If we are honest, we will admit that this is a subject we must deal with eventually.

There are four broad categories that people tend to fall into when asked, "Does God exist?" These are not types of religions, but rather, viewpoints that clarify their position on the existence of God. Within each viewpoint, people will differ on the details. I will not attempt to exhaustively look at all these details, but simply give an overview and my thoughts to promote consideration of each.

The starting point on the evolution of faith is atheism. Atheism is a lack of belief in God. Many atheists would say that since we cannot see or touch God, he does not exist. He is simply a figment of our imagination. They would say that people use God as a crutch to deal with the difficulties in life in an effort to find some comfort.

However, this leaves them in a difficult place when attempting to answer some very big questions in life. Why do we exist? Does life have a purpose? Where did the universe come from?

It's not that atheists have no faith. They simply choose to place their faith in something other than God. Atheists tend to look to science for their answers. In that sense, science is their replacement for God. But, is science a worthy god? Let's examine this.

Science is the method by which we discover our universe. In that role, it is very useful. Through science, we have gained insight into how our bodies and the world around us function, and ways we can take advantage of this. We have discovered lifesaving medicines and harnessed the power of the atom. We have made our species flourish using science.

But science is simply a tool—a cold, calculated, often tedious process. While it has enormous usefulness, science can't replace God. Unlike God, science is not the Creator. You may say, "But what about all the advances of science, including the technology, understanding, and skills which have moved the human race forward and made so many lives better?" This is true, but science does not have the ability to create *something from nothing*. Science instead finds ways to utilize the things that God has already provided for us. It is creative but not the Creator.

So, I would propose that science's proper place is to help us discover our Creator as we examine his creation.

Also, science, in and of itself, is amoral. In fact, this is necessary to have outcomes that are not slanted in one way or another. At times, scientists will bring their morality into it, whether for better or for worse. However, science itself is not looking for moral results but rather greater knowledge.

With science as their god, atheists, therefore, choose to have no objective moral standard to guide them. They can choose their own subjective morality, but then nothing is absolute. This is quite disturbing when you consider some of the things that have been done in the name of science. Without God, everything, including humans, can be reduced to something to be studied and our intrinsic worth is diminished. So, when atheism elevates science to a god-like status, they are in danger of losing their moral grounding.

I know that atheists do not want my sympathy, but I find it sad that they place their faith in the science-god. James Freeman Clarke once said, "He who never looks up to a living God, to a heavenly presence, loses the power of perceiving that presence, and the universe slowly turns into a dead machine, clashing and grinding on, without purpose or end. If the light within us is darkness, how great is that darkness!"[1]

Someone unfamiliar with the Bible might believe that its authors spend some time and effort defending against atheism and proving the existence of God. They don't. One verse sums up the Biblical attitude toward it.

> *The fool says in his heart there is no God. —Ps 14:1*

After atheism comes agnosticism. This belief system says, "There may be a god, but we just cannot know." Since they cannot be certain, they remain on the theological fence and make no choice about the existence of God. Of course, if we knew for sure,

1. Gilbert, *Dictionary of Burning Words*, 563.

there would no longer be any need for faith. Faith would be replaced by fact and our journey would end.

But, in making no choice agnostics *are* choosing. You can go no further up or down the path without first hopping off the fence. In practice, agnostics are atheists because it does not make sense to take any time or expend any energy understanding or relating to a god that may or may not exist. They are therefore refusing any relationality that might come from choosing God.

The next step in our evolution of faith is deism. Deism holds that there is a God who created the universe but that he does not intervene in human affairs. Further, it says that God has never given us any special revelation about himself, only what we can see of him from his creation. So, a deists would not put any stock in what the Bible says about God, claiming that it is simply the musings of men.

Deism can be thought of as a theological "safe bet." This premise accepts the fact of God as our creator—which they would say is so clearly seen in the existence, order, beauty, and complexity of nature—but balks at any further definition. Defining God further would be risky because who is to say that one man's opinion of God is any better than the next?

The most widely used illustration of the deistic approach is that of the watchmaker. God, in this view, is a creator and artisan, much like a man who crafts a watch. The watchmaker god winds up the universe he has made, takes a step back and allows it to run its course, not interfering in the process. This makes the entire universe a celestial experiment that God simply observes.

The problem with this view is what it leaves on the table. There is a limit to how much we can learn about God through his creation. So much about God, his characteristics, and his relationship to his creation, is only hinted at by that which he created. So, deists also pass on sharing in much of his relationality.

Imagine you have in your hands the most sophisticated phone ever created. It has innumerable awesome apps and is as powerful as the best supercomputers. It has an almost endless memory and a lightning fast processor. The battery will go on for weeks without dropping past 90 percent. The camera takes movies like a professional studio. Its speakers sound like you are sitting in the front row of a concert. It has awesome gadgets galore all tucked away in a sleek design. But its owner ignores all those sweet capabilities and simply uses it to make phone calls and send the occasional text.

Most of us would say that would be a sad waste. The deist is viewing God in the same manner as that phone's owner, having no concept of what could be. This is all because they cannot accept the possibility that God may be interacting and communicating with his creation.

This brings us to theism. It is the final step in the Evolution of Faith. Theism contends that God is more than just a distant creator of the universe. Not only does God communicate, he intervenes in his creation and sustains a relationship with his creatures. The proof of this is mainly found in special revelation called scriptures. Any theist has made a leap of faith that God has spoken to us and related more about who he is. But this leap is really more like a hop. There is good reason to believe God has spoken to his creation. Let's quickly explore this notion.

We saw earlier through our little word game that pretty much everything relates in some way to other things. Since all creation is relational, it follows logically that the God who created everything must be relational. A central part of a relational being is communication. Would this highly relational God want to remain silent throughout history just watching from afar? That doesn't make sense to me. How about you?

Think about new parents. They have their first baby and fall madly in love with the little tyke. They record every coo and smile and celebrate every developmental step. They can't wait to tell people about what the little one is up to. Wouldn't it be very curious if about the time their baby starts learning to talk, they chose to not talk back, but instead, watch silently from afar?

The same should be true of God. He created every person who has ever lived. In that sense, we are all God's children. Above all the animals, God has given us the ability to communicate at a high level both spoken and written. What sense would it make for him to never communicate with his children using the skills he has given us? Perhaps it is the very reason God gave us these abilities.

Since the qualifications to be a theist are simply to believe in a god (or gods) and believe that god communicates with us, there are many types of theism. Most organized religions would be considered theistic and it is probably what you think when you hear the phrase, "people of faith."

If you are searching, all these theistic choices can easily become overwhelming and confusing. So here is something that might help. The thing it comes down to is deciding what *is* special revelation from God and what *is not*. What has God truly said about himself? I hope this book helps you find a good answer to that question, but the good news is that you do not have to do this alone. Just ask God to take the journey with you.

As you read about the Evolution of Faith, did you give some thought to where you would land on this scale? Are you an atheist, agnostic, deist, or theist? It is an exercise worth doing. To have never considered such an important aspect of the human experience would be unfortunate. There is a saying that is often attributed to Mark Twain that rings true to me: "The two most important days in your life are the day you are born and the day you find out why."[2]

Consider for a moment how profound it would be to find out why you were born; to understand why you exist. This journey into faith can give you the answer, because surely the "why" must come from the one who created you. Let me give you a glimpse into this.

I recently watched a Ted Talk titled, "Everything You Think You Know About Addiction is Wrong" which described a new way to look at addiction.[3] I was interested in the video because I spent ten years working at a drug and alcohol treatment center. I wanted to see if this video had new insights, and I was not disappointed.

The presenter, Johann Hari, described the main cause of addiction as disconnection. In this view, an addict "disconnects" from aspects of their life they find too painful. They use drugs to avoid these harsh realities. But, because of the negative consequences of

2. Seybold, "The Apocryphal Twain," para. 2.

3. TedGlobalLondon. "Everything you think you know about addiction".

drug usage, they begin to spiral downward until the drug is the only part of life they care about, having lost any positive aspects they might have once had.

Hari then argued that the best treatment for an addict is to teach them how to deal with the more difficult aspects of life and reintroduce worthwhile and meaningful connections. These can be found in the purpose of hobbies or careers, but more importantly, in relationships to others, where they find a sense of belonging and affirmation. With these in place, any need to use drugs would be diminished as they begin to enjoy their lives and decide they would not want to lose these new bonds.

Addiction is a nuanced issue, but Hari's contention about the importance of meaningful connections seems to hit on a basic truth about humanity. We need positive, loving relationship in our lives. But I would take that one step further. What if a person not only connected to the healthy things in life and to beneficial relationships, but also to their creator? Surely a deep bond with the loving God, who fashioned all the good things in life, would have the most potential to change a person for the better?

So, when we begin to explore God, we have the chance to find some compelling answers and pleasing consequences. But, as you travel the road of faith, there are a couple of potholes that I would like to help you avoid. Maybe it will make your journey a bit less bumpy.

How *Not* to Find God

It is part of man's nature to wonder about his creator. This is one reason why religion has always been a part of human society. Our urge to find God can end with us finding purpose, identity, and values that take us far beyond what we find in everyday life. It can answer the deeper questions about life and the afterlife. So, the answers we discover are very important. And, being misled can have weighty consequences.

Interestingly, our search for God is also a relational path, mainly because we are not looking for a thing; we are looking for a person. Let's imagine that you are a private investigator hired to track down a missing person. What steps would you take to begin your search?

A good investigator would want to gather as much information as possible about the person for whom they are searching. What do they look like? Who did they hang out with? Where do they work? What are their hobbies? You would spend hours looking at photos, poring over personal information, and interviewing people to put together a profile of the person in question. In your search, you would become an expert on your missing person. Strangely enough, without ever having met them, you would know them better than many of the people in their life.

When we learn about people, we naturally want to get to know who they *really* are. But, for some reason, when we start exploring God, most of us take a different route and make a couple of major mistakes. Both mistakes center around opinions. Let's consider these mistakes and learn how *not* to find God.

The first mistake is taking other people's opinions about God as fact without checking to see if these opinions have any validity. Do you already have some beliefs about God? Ok, great. How did you get them? Seriously. What are your beliefs built upon? Was it handed to you as a system of faith or did you explore yourself? Did you take the time to consider it critically, or simply accept it without question?

Maybe you took on your parent's faith out of a sense of duty because you didn't want to rock the boat or strain your family ties. But there is a real problem with this. You see, there is no such thing as a second-hand relationship. To know God, *you* must know God.

I am sure that many people reading this would consider themselves Christians. So, let me address you for a moment. You may have learned what you know of God by going to church on Sunday and listening to your pastor preach. He may be a rather nice, well-meaning person. But what did you do to test the validity of the sermons? Did you simply accept what was said, or did you do the work of checking and evaluating them against what the Bible says?

Another way to ask this would be: has your mind and heart been engaged in the pursuit and clarification of your beliefs? If not, you are simply going through the motions and being spoon-fed information that may or may not be accurate. You are trusting another person's opinion.

In telling you this, I am not just giving out advice. I learned the hard way. I attended a church for years that I was very fond of which had a pastor who was a gifted teacher. He could open the Bible, bring out its truths and help you apply them to your life better than most pastors I had heard. I trusted what he was saying completely, never dreaming he may have had ulterior motives.

For the most part, my trust was well-grounded. My pastor was theologically sound, and his teachings helped me grow as a young Christian. But, in one area that he was passionate about, he sharply departed from what the Bible clearly taught. Moreover, he tried to twist scripture to support his opinion and then taught this to the church congregation. This brought about changes in the structure and leadership of the church that were unbiblical.

When I finally realized what was happening, I felt betrayed and foolish for not having sensed what he was doing much earlier. But I learned a valuable lesson. I now know what I should have done to keep from being fooled.

The book of Acts in the Bible gives us a perfect example of how we should approach this. The apostle Paul goes to a group of Jews in an area called Berea. He begins to preach the Gospel of Jesus Christ to them. Check out how they react.

> *Now the Bereans were of more noble character than the Thessalonians, for they received the message with great eagerness and examined the Scriptures every day to see if what Paul said was true. —Acts 17:10*

Did you catch that? They did not take Paul's word for it. They scoured the scriptures themselves to see if it lined up with what they were being told. Far from being chastised for it, the Bible says that they were more noble for doing so!

Even as I write this, I am keenly aware of the fact that I am giving you my opinion and asking you to follow my advice. Should you trust me? Actually, no. Although I will do my level best to fairly present evidence to support my hypothesis that God is relational, I am not asking nor expecting you to place your trust in me. You should do the work yourself. I would argue that it should be the same for any faith system. If it does not hold up to scrutiny, it is not worth holding onto.

Maybe you grew up in a home where God was never mentioned, or he was even maligned as being false. What should you do? First, thanks for picking up a book about God. That shows a level of curiosity and initiative. Perhaps God was prompting you. Second, I would tell you the same thing. Don't take your parent's or anyone else's word for it. Do the work yourself. Begin to explore the best resources and ask God to join you in the search.

When we engage our hearts and minds in the pursuit of truth, what we end up finding will not just be a list of factoids. We will have the potential of internalizing what we learn and walking away from the experience a changed person with real convictions.

The other mistake you can often make when considering God is trusting *your own* opinion. That is, don't just make stuff up. So many times, I have heard statements like, "I can't believe in a god who would judge someone. My god wouldn't do that." Or, "My god wouldn't tell me it is wrong to have sex outside of marriage. He just wants me to be happy." These types of statements reflect the idea that everyone gets to make up their own personal god.

Instead of finding out who God truly is, many people will project what they want onto God for their own selfish reasons. I think the temptation to do this comes from the hiddenness of God. Since we can't see him, we think we can just make him up.

If we wanted, we could begin to give God all sorts of imaginary characteristics. We could make believe that God is a giant on top of the tallest mountain. A person can only get to him through great personal effort and when you get there, the giant could be dangerous! Or, we could decide that he is like a genie in a bottle who will give us three wishes if we rub the lamp. Like the ancient Greeks, we could create a pantheon of Gods who look and act a whole lot like humans on a television soap opera but with much more power.

I hope you are beginning to see the problem. When we use our imagination to make up a god, there is no evidence that any of the things we believe are true. Our beliefs will also contradict the beliefs of others. Please hear me say this: just because you or I believe something does not make it true. The foolishness of this is that we try to create our creator, and of course, that is a backward approach.

Let's look at this in a practical way. What if a co-worker who barely knows you began making claims about you? You hear from others that he called you a racist and claimed you stole money from the company. You would have every right to be upset about this because this co-worker would be slandering you. To slander a person means to make a damaging or false statement about them. If you do this with God, it is far worse. Slandering God is called blasphemy and is the act of insulting or showing contempt or lack of reverence toward God. Making things up about who he is falls under that category.

Before I knew God, I did this myself. As a young man musing about who he was, I would cobble together interesting concepts, pop psychology, and things people had told me along with ideas and desires of my own and call this Frankenstein creation of mine "god." Not surprisingly, this god thought just like me and was rather accepting of my poor behavior. He was more concerned with my happiness than anything else and would change to fit the occasion. Perhaps you have done something similar?

Compare that with what God says of himself in the Bible:

> *"For my thoughts are not your thoughts, neither are your ways my ways," declares the Lord. "As the heavens are higher than the earth, so are my ways higher than your ways and my thoughts than your thoughts."* —*Isa 55:8–9*

Quite the contrast. We cannot make up God because God already *is*. So, if we want to get to know who he is, we need to find him and ask him.

Eventually I realized how wrong I was. I set aside my Frankenstein god and became passionately interested in discovering who he really is. That was right around the time that I met him.

So, having looked at two ways not to find God, how then should we proceed? We have already talked about the hiddenness of God. How does one get to know an invisible God? I'm glad I asked.

There are many things we know about God without turning to opinions or imagination. They are found in two broad categories. The first is called general revelation and the second is called special revelation.

General revelation is what we can learn about God from his creation. Much like you can see the heart and mind of an artist in their paintings, we discover our creator in all the beauty and intricacies of the universe he crafted. The stars and planets, oceans and mountains, animals and plants all have a story to tell. They reflect the face of the one who made them.

As awesome as nature is, it cannot answer all our questions about God. The only way we could find out things like his name, what he expects from us, or his plan for creation is if he told us himself. That is where special revelation comes in. We do not need to rely upon anyone's opinion about God when we have God's opinion.

When something is believed to be a special revelation from God, it is called scripture. Scripture guides us deeper into understanding the truths that the human heart longs to understand. In them we find that there is something beyond this physical world and temporary life. We can peek behind the curtain and see spiritual mysteries revealed.

As you can probably tell, I believe the Bible is truly the only special revelation from God. A little later, we will look at this claim more closely. Until then I will simply say that as one explores the Bible with God, everything about him shines through.

Both these avenues are so much better than making things up or taking half-baked truths from secondhand sources. We will be considering each starting with general revelation. But first, I need to clarify some terms I will be using.

Because we will look at relationality in different forms and in differing degrees, you need to be familiar with the following definitions. I hope this helps show the difference between how two stones relate as compared to two people. Let's start with the simplest of the three: categorical.

Categorical relationships would be those that fit together. Remember Sesame Street? To teach the kids about the same and different, they would show four objects and start the song that went, "One of these things is not like the others, one of these things just isn't the same . . ." (You will have to imagine the music.) With categorical relationships, it is simply putting things together that belong together. This might seem overly simplistic, but all the order that we take for granted—the patterns that help us make sense of the universe—had to come from somewhere. I am sure I can say that categorically.

The second type of relationality is interconnectedness. We can see this best in nature. All the animals and plants in a given area are interconnected. They are all adapted to live with and off each other. They need each other. The zebra needs the grass created by the monsoons in Africa. Birds need trees to build their nests. The polar bear needs the ice flow to hunt. The blue whale needs the krill to munch on. Across the face of the earth, nature is uniquely and deeply interconnected.

Finally, there is interacting. It can be defined as acting in such a way as to connect with others. This is what generally comes to mind when we think of relationships. It is social behavior like deer fawns frolicking together. It is two wild dog packs fighting over territory. It is also a group of people chatting over a cup of coffee. Humans interact constantly. Whether it is navigating traffic driving to work or discussing the nuances of good parenting, we are highly social creatures. I would submit that in this we are reflecting our creator.

Keep these terms in mind as we journey into God's relationality.

SECTION TWO

General Revelation

God in His Creation

Categorical Relationships and the Fabric of Reality

How long has it been since you looked up into the night sky? I don't mean a glance; I mean lying back and spending some real time soaking up the beauty of the heavens above on a clear night. As I have already said, my hometown of Canyon is small and flat. I moved to the Dallas area to go to college and have been around the metroplex ever since. I have enjoyed this area, but it is full of cities and developments and is spread out over miles and miles. With all the tall buildings and artificial light from so many different sources, it affects the clarity of the night sky. On one of my trips back home, I realized how strikingly different it is in a rural area.

Yes, Canyon is small and flat, but that makes for a wide-open night sky with the stars shining brilliantly above without competition from man-made luminescence. It can be truly breathtaking on a crisp fall evening when the moon is full. The vista just goes on and on. I can't help but think about God and sense a connection as I watch this spectacle. The same God who created that panorama also created me.

In the heavens above, his craftsmanship is on full display and humans are the only one of his creatures on earth that can really appreciate this as a work of art. It feels like he did it just for us to enjoy. Do yourself a favor and check it out sometime soon. It can kick-start your sense of wonder.

I do not know if there is life elsewhere in the universe, but I would still contend that the cosmos is full of relationships. This type of relationship has to do with the constants that can be found anywhere you look in the heavens. It is the connectedness and order of the planets, stars, and galaxies.

Although it may look like the stars are just random dots in the sky, we know that they are so much more. In actuality, the universe is extremely orderly. Science has looked deeply into the universe and found the laws that make it work. There is no argument between science, philosophy, and theology about the existence of the natural laws. Science does its best to explain them, philosophy asks, "Where did the laws come from?" and theology tells us there is an answer.

One such law is the law of universal gravitation. Without gravity, matter would not bind together to form masses. A star has form because it has a gravitational force holding it together. That force also affects objects near enough to it, moving them towards the star. A planet has its own smaller gravitational force. Although it is pulled towards a star, the planet's gravitational force generally keeps it from being drawn completely into the star. It finds its orbit around a star when the push and pull of the two gravitational forces find their balancing point.

This is how the larger universe is ordered. Most galaxies have a black hole at the center that has a massive gravitational force.[1] The gravity of the black hole eventually overpowers the gravitational force of the stars in that galaxy. This causes the stars to collectively form amazing spiral patterns (not unlike a whirlpool) that are moving very slowly towards the middle. Fortunately for the stars, this process can take billions of years to complete. In turn, the planets find their orbits around the stars and moons around planets.

The law of gravitation is a powerful force that puts everything in space in its place. Because the universe is designed in this way, there can be sensible categorical relationships. So, when you look up into the night sky, the order created by gravity enables you to know that the Milky Way is there and stable, and the constellation Orion is going to be where it is supposed to within it.

1. NASA Science. "Black Holes," para. 7.

Did you know that scientifically, there is no definitive proof of gravity? In other words, it is impossible to fill a bottle with gravity, point at it and say, "Here is gravity. It definitely exists." We know it is there because of its observable effects on the things around it. Even though it is a foundational law of our universe, science cannot go beyond simply describing this effect. Why does gravity act the way it does? Why does it even exist? The skeptic would say that one day science will know the answer. The believer says that we know already.

Gravity is only one of the amazing things that we take for granted every day. We do not have to worry about floating off into space because gravity keeps us anchored to the earth. It is part of the fabric of reality that makes it possible to live and helps us make sense of everything around us. At times, there are small tears in the fabric of reality; anomalies that are not easy to explain. But, by and large, we are presented with a reality that we can logically sort out and utilize to navigate our existence.

Logic itself is a fascinating part of the fabric of reality. For some reason, we have reason. We can infer things about reality, and because of the constants of our universe, we can get it right. Simple things like the fact that water is wet and light drives away the darkness. If we see something in the light, there is actually something there. Our senses are correct the great majority of the time. They are fine-tuned to our surroundings. If it is sweet, we tasted sugar. If it is soft, we touched velvet. If we hear the word "hello," there is someone greeting us.

But logic goes far beyond these basics. Like Sherlock Holmes, we can use our logic to deduce things. The sun came up yesterday and every day before that. It is logical to assume that the pattern will continue, and the sun will come out tomorrow. We are so certain of it we write songs about it. We can understand that a person has been on the trail before us by the footprints she leaves behind. We can make a connection between tears and feelings.

Moreover, we can create and invent. A tree is converted into boards to build a house. Metal is forged to create the parts of an engine and we determine what fuel will make it run. Colorful pigments are skillfully brushed on canvas and artwork is created. We can postulate and communicate. We create words and then put them into writing. Written words become a sentence. Several sentences become a paragraph and many paragraphs later we have a book. Others can read that book and understand the thoughts of the author.

All this should be astonishing. Our reason makes sense of the reality we are in. Yet, we take it all for granted. We almost never ask why it makes sense. Where did the fabric of reality come from, and why can we interact with it so well?

With our logical minds we put everything into categories. And, conversely, in an orderly universe, most everything can be categorized. Simply put, a tree is a tree and a rock, a rock. All trees can be categorized in a group called trees and all rocks can be similarly grouped. This is relational because a tree on the other side of the world is a tree and a rock on the other side of the universe is a rock. Because these categories hold true, all trees or rocks can be said to relate to each other through their similar traits. For example, if we know what an oak tree is, we can see a beech tree for the first time and categorize it as a tree.

As we identify and categorize things, we can see how they relate to each other and to the things around them. A large pile of similar rocks can be called a hill. A large hill is a mountain. If you have a big enough pile of rocks held together by a gravitational force, you have a moon or a planet. In this sense, the rocks all relate to one another to form something else. This is, of course, a big oversimplification, but the point is to show relationships at the most basic level. These categories are the simplest form of relating. It can be done with almost anything in the universe.

We can order things by their similarity *and* their differences. Even apparent opposites can be categorized and show relationships. What is light without darkness? What is close if there is not distant? A rainy day would mean little if there were not sunny days to contrast. The concept of cold would not exist unless there was heat for comparison. All these things relate in their oppositeness.

Perhaps this is becoming tedious to you. You know this already. I am basically going back over things you learned as a preschooler. I understand, but my objective in this is threefold. First, to help you see past this reality we live in being a mundane, everyday fact. When it is brought to the forefront, the order of the universe is awe-inspiring.

Second, I want to show you this is exceedingly relational. All our categories fit together, and a web of relationality is formed that enables us to understand our reality. Order enables categories, categories enable logical deductions, deductions enable us to build an understanding of reality.

Third, it all points to something bigger. Remember our glow-in-the-dark God? As you ponder how all this order could be, he begins to shine. A person who considers the origin of the fabric of reality only has two choices. Either all this happened by accident, mindlessly developing into a deeply comprehensible system, or there is a mind behind it, putting it all together for us in a way that points back to him.

Let me expand on this by going back to gravity for a moment. I stated earlier that even though we can't directly observe it, we know gravity is there because of its powerful, observable effects on the things around it. Because of these effects, gravity is a certainty. This is true of God. He seems hidden, but as you examine what he has done in creation, and how he continues to affect it, he becomes undeniable. Denying God is therefore comparable to a person rejecting gravity or other immaterial things, such as love or dreams, simply because these cannot be held in our hands.

Perhaps I have not yet done a good enough job of showing God in all this. Let's look at one more example that I hope will bring it home. You may need to sharpen your pencil for this one.

There is nothing like mathematics in the rest of creation. It is unique. To use mathematical vernacular, it is singular. It has many characteristics which can be found nowhere else. Let's explore mathematics and see if we can learn more about God.

Mathematics can be described as one of the purest things in the universe. There is almost nothing vague about it. Math always brings you to a black and white answer. One plus one equals two every time. It can be used to succinctly describe the physical universe. This means that the fabric of the universe is stitched together mathematically.

Mathematical concepts such as distance, weight, height, mass, velocity, and circumference all help us to understand the place in which we exist. Not only does our universe become easier to describe with math, but as you go deeper into reality, it becomes the only way to describe it. At the quantum level, math describes things that would otherwise be too small to comprehend.

There is something very attractive about this unmessy part of science. It is satisfying to do an equation and get the exact right answer with no uncertainty. With this, math can be used to show that the universe is not only orderly, but precise. There are many things about our world that must be exactly right for life to be sustained. One such measurement is the orbit of our planet. We have already examined how gravity is responsible for establishing the orbit of a planet around a star. But with the orbit of the Earth around the Sun, gravity is extremely precise.

As the Earth moves in its orbit around the Sun, it departs from a straight line by only one-ninth of an inch every eighteen miles. If it departed by one-eighth of an inch, we would come so close to the Sun that we would be incinerated; if it departed by one-tenth of an inch, we would find ourselves so far from the Sun that we would all freeze to death.[2]

Another finely tuned constant is the strong nuclear force or the force that holds atoms together. Stars burn by fusing hydrogen. When two hydrogen atoms fuse, 0.7% of the mass of the hydrogen is converted into energy. If the amount converted were 0.6%, there would not be enough for a proton to bond to a neutron. The universe would then consist of hydrogen and there would be no oxygen. If the amount of matter converted were 0.8%, fusion would happen so fast that no hydrogen would have survived from the beginnings of the universe. The number must lie exactly between

2. Science Digest.

0.6% and 0.8% for our universe to have hydrogen and oxygen existing together.[3]

These are just two examples of an amazing abundance of precision that become apparent when mathematics is applied to our cosmos. But, let's spend some time just focusing on mathematics itself. The very fact that there is such a thing as math is crazy orderly. So much so, it is our main tool for describing order.

Think for a moment about numbers. Each one has its place in line. Read the first few:

1 2 4 3 5 6 7 8 9

Did you notice the discrepancy? Because the order of the numbers is so well established, we all know that the three and four need to be switched. There is actually a myriad of ways to order the numbers other than ascending numeric values, but the key word is *order*.

Without order, mathematics would be useless. If every equation had a random answer, there would be no point in doing equations. Not only do numbers facilitate order, they provide proof of the order that exists. Math shows us orderliness as each equation completes with one correct answer out of the countless incorrect ones.

This leads naturally to the question, why is there so much order? Why is it so prevalent in the fabric of reality? Why isn't the universe instead ruled by chaos? That would surely be the case if the universe simply randomly existed. The high level of order in mathematics and the way it demonstrates order in the rest of the universe suggests that its existence isn't random.

There is a debate that has been raging in the world of mathematics for centuries. The question is, was mathematics invented or discovered? The answer to this question is important because it indicates whether math is a creation of man or of God. If invented, then it is a purely man-made construct that we developed to better understand our universe. If it was discovered, that means it preexisted man and must have come from another source.

3. Rees, *Just Six Numbers*, 49.

Albert Einstein once remarked, "How can it be that mathematics, being after all a product of human thought which is independent of experience, is so admirably appropriate to the objects of reality?"[4] Perhaps the answer to this deep question is that mathematics isn't simply a product of human thought.

There are aspects of math that are obviously man-made. We came up with the symbols that represent numbers and equations. We came up with ways to apply these equations to the world around us. But even the most ardent supporter of the idea that math is man-made must admit that there are truths about mathematics that would be true even if man had never done a single calculation.

One plus one equals two. That simple equation and all other equations are true regardless of man's use of it. It was true at the beginning of time and it will continue to be true when there is not a human left on earth. This truth is independent of man.

As well, each human society discovered math at different times and under different circumstances, and yet, math is completely consistent no matter who is using it. Unlike language, which developed differently in each culture, mathematics is identical in its nature across all cultures. Addition works the same way for everyone. It is a universal truth. It is so consistent that science calls these truths *laws*.

So, man could not have invented but only *discovered* these truths. We are then left with the question, where did the laws of mathematics come from? Simply put, laws come from a lawmaker.

The laws of mathematics are a convincing argument for the existence of God, but they go even further. In fact, they are so perfect and orderly that they approach God-like characteristics.

Vern Poythress is a first-class mathematician with a PhD from Harvard in mathematics. He is of the opinion that math must originate from the mind of God. In his book, Redeeming Mathematics, he explores this assertion by showing how characteristics generally attributed to God are also true of mathematics.

4. Ellis, "Geometry and Experience," para. 2.

Poythress argues that mathematical laws—to be properly relied upon—must have attributes which indicate an origin in God.[5] Let's briefly look at some of these attributes.

Mathematical laws *must be true everywhere*. This is much like the omnipresence of God, being present everywhere at the same time. They *must be true always* showing they are eternally unchanging like the Biblical description of God in Hebrews 13:8.

Like God, these laws can also be thought of as *all-powerful* in that there is no power in the universe that can change two plus two into something other than four. As well, numbers reflect *eternity* in that they can go on infinitely.

Therefore, math doesn't simply show the need for a lawmaker, it reflects the character of the lawmaker like nothing else in this universe. Poythress expressed it like this: "When God created the world, he also ordained all the characteristics of the world. It is he who specifies all the truths about the world, including the truths of mathematics."[6]

Now let's tie this into the premise of this book. Can the mathematical truths created by God also show his relationality? The answer is a resounding *yes* because math is a form of communication. Science is built upon the foundation set by math. If not for math, the rest of science could not be quantified. So, in this sense, math is a language. In fact, math is so crystal clear, it is a universal language. When information is related using math, it is perfectly understood—nothing lacking in the translation.

So, when one scientist wants to communicate with another, math is the preferred method. A scientist in India can communicate mathematically to a Brazilian scientist and be perfectly understood. And, of course, communication is a foundational part of relationality. Try and have a relationship with someone without communicating with them. It wouldn't be long before that relationship would be dead.

In considering categorical relationships, we have discovered that the order of the universe presents us with a reality that can

5. Bowyer, "God In Mathematics." para. 4.

6. Poythress, *Redeeming Mathematics*, 185.

be categorized. These sensible categories allow us to use reason to interact with our surroundings. In creating order, God shows that he is intimately involved in the details of his creation and even at its mathematical core, his universe is relational.

Given this fabric of reality as a backdrop, we will move on and explore the next level of God's relationality. Let's explore just how interconnected this amazing creation is.

Interconnectedness of Life

THERE IS A FAMOUS image taken by the Voyager 1 space probe from about 3.76 billion miles away from where it was launched. In it, you can see a vast expanse of space and a tiny blue speck that is almost indiscernible. That speck is the earth looking no bigger than a grain of sand. Carl Sagan, the famous astronomer, cosmologist and astrophysicist, commenting on that photo in a speech said:

> Look again at that dot. That's here. That's home. That's us. On it everyone you love, everyone you know, everyone you ever heard of, every human being who ever was, lived out their lives. The aggregate of our joy and suffering, thousands of confident religions, ideologies, and economic doctrines, every hunter and forager, every hero and coward, every creator and destroyer of civilization, every king and peasant, every young couple in love, every mother and father, hopeful child, inventor and explorer, every teacher of morals, every corrupt politician, every "superstar," every "supreme leader," every saint and sinner in the history of our species lived there-on a mote of dust suspended in a sunbeam . . . Our posturings, our imagined self-importance, the delusion that we have some privileged position in the Universe, are challenged by this point of pale light. Our planet is a lonely speck in the great enveloping cosmic dark. In our obscurity, in all this vastness, there is no hint that help will come from elsewhere to save us from ourselves."[1]

1. Sagan, *Pale Blue Dot*, 6–7.

If you look at the entirety of the speech, you will see that Dr. Sagan had positive intentions. He was stating that we need to come together as humans, stop fighting and take care of our world since it is the only one we have. But this positive note can easily get lost when it is taken from the materialistic, scientific viewpoint. Materialism is the belief that there is nothing spiritual, but only those things that can be seen and empirically studied.

Carl Sagan was also famously atheistic in his beliefs. Although he ultimately denied being an atheist, his leanings appeared to be those of an agnostic who was quite sure there was no god. What he is describing is that the earth is no different from the rest of the universe. In fact, in comparison to the vastness surrounding it, our world is tiny and insignificant and could be easily snuffed out. Apparently, there is nothing that can save us from our self-imposed, impending doom. Depressed yet?

I certainly do not want to leave my readers in such a place of utter insignificance and hopelessness. So, perhaps I can help you get over your despair. Is there something to our "imagined self-importance"? Is it possible that we have "some privileged position in the universe"? Yes. All I need to do is show you that the earth is not just like the rest of the universe. It is actually very special. I can do that in one word: life.

Sagan briefly mentions life on earth at another point in this speech but does not stop to consider how completely unique this makes us from the rest of the known universe. The contrast is stunning. As we have looked out as far as we can, all that is seen in space is emptiness, lifeless chunks of rock, and burning energy sources. Space appears dead and sterile.

But not here. Not only is there life, the earth is absolutely exploding with it. Everywhere you go, from the highest mountains to the deepest parts of the ocean, life dominates. The vastness and variety of life is stunning. Science has already discovered and categorized millions of different species and, as our ability to recognize life at the micro level increases, that number should grow into the billions.

In his diatribe, Sagan goes on describing how all human affairs have begun and ended on earth. What he looks right past is the fact that humans *exist*. As remarkable as life on earth is, humans are even more extraordinary in our unique abilities. In our intelligence and inventiveness, passions and morality, communication and self-awareness, we stand alone. Considering this, we humans are distinctly above the rest of creation. Our acceptance of this is not a product of "self-importance," it is simply self-evident.

It would be easy enough to make the claim that we are the only known planet in the universe that has life and play that as a trump card. Although that is true, we need to go a bit deeper because it is not a particularly robust claim. We have yet to scratch the surface in our capability to detect life on other planets. In the known universe, there are billions of galaxies and trillions of stars. Planets are harder for us to see and thus hard to calculate, but there are certainly more planets than stars. So, surely there are a vast number of planets that could be friendly to life?

Let's examine that for a moment. Science seems fond of telling us how simple it is to create and sustain life. All you need is light, water, and a simple mix of chemicals and *poof*—you have life. But is that true? With our best scientific efforts, we certainly have not been able to produce it. Even here on a planet that is perfect for sustaining life. We have modified life to some degree and even created clones, but the fact is, life has never been seen to come from non-life. If it does not happen here in a world full of life with the assistance of the greatest scientific minds, why is it assumed that life has popped up all over the universe on its own?

The very fact that the earth is a *blue* dot with a life sustaining atmosphere makes it stand out from every other dot we have ever discovered. That striking blueness is the reason that you can pick out the earth in the photo taken from 3.76 billion miles away. As well, our atmosphere is only one factor among many that makes life possible on earth. Earth has been called a "goldilocks" planet due to the fact that there are so many factors that make it just right for life.[2] Although opinions on what should be on this list varies,

2. Zalasiewicz and Williams, *The Goldilocks Planet*, 1–2.

each factor adds tremendously to the long odds of any other planet being enough like earth to sustain life as we know it. Whether it is our orbit around the sun, large enough moon and neighboring planets, correct planetary mass, molten core, steady plate tectonics, rocky surface, or the tilt of our axis, we become mathematically more and more singular.

Interestingly, one of the factors happens to be our star being in the proper place in the Milky Way Galaxy.[3] We are apparently near the edge of our galaxy, about two-thirds away from the center. This is an optimal place to be. As you get closer to the center of the Milky Way, it becomes much more crowded with stars because of the enormous black hole at the center drawing them in. Our position means less chance of collisions with the crowd of celestial bodies, less interference from other gravitational forces and a much safer distance from the influence of the black hole. So, our sun and planet are literally in a "privileged position in the universe".

Having said all this, there may be life somewhere else in the universe. It is unimaginably vast, and we simply do not know. But that would only mean that there are other very privileged and special planets that have been similarly blessed by our creator.

Just as the cosmos are arranged, life on earth is orderly. In life, we begin to see the depth of the relationality of God. We see it in ecosystems. The term ecosystem can be defined as a biological community of interacting organisms within their environment.

As you could learn in any elementary school textbook on biology, there is a large diversity of ecosystems including forests and grasslands, rivers and oceans, deserts and arctic tundra. There is the living (biotic) part of an ecosystem and the non-living (abiotic) part. The biotic includes the plants and animals, and the abiotic includes the water and land. In space, there cannot be an ecosystem because, as far as we know, only the abiotic exists.

What truly makes an ecosystem is how the different elements interact. There is a high level of reliance between the organisms, their environment, and the other creatures. Without rocks, no soil can be produced. Without soil, plants cannot grow. Without

3. Institute for Creation Research, "Earth Was Created," para. 4.

plants, herbivores have nothing to eat. Without herbivores, carnivores have no sustenance. Without water, everything perishes.

These interconnections are often so deep and intricate that symbiosis occurs. Mutual symbiosis is when two dissimilar organisms are in intimate, interdependent association which increase chances of survival. Often, they cannot subsist without each other. Symbiosis is quite common. We humans have a symbiotic relationship with the flora and fauna that live in our digestive tract that help us digest food. The clownfish lives among the sea anemone and both are better protected. The koala and the eucalyptus tree both benefit as the koala gets its food and the tree gets pruned regularly.

You may say, "Of course this is the case. That is just how everything works." But, why? Consider for a moment a world where there is life but little to no interconnectedness. Imagine that each life form has its own area that includes all the elements necessary to exist but separated from other life forms. Given that this is a real possibility, there seems to be little reason why life forms would need to interact. Each one could just live out its life individually, independent from the rest.

This, however, isn't how life works. We find instead a world where being separate is by far the exception to the rule. From apex predator to microorganism, everything here is linked.

This is true to the extent that if you remove a link from an ecosystem it can fundamentally change or even decimate the ecology. I found a very interesting example of this in a video on YouTube. The title is "How Wolves Change Rivers."[4] Intrigued, I clicked on it and learned a fascinating story.

Wolves had been gone from the Yellowstone area for around 70 years, having been eradicated or driven off by hunters worried about the safety of their families and livestock. Due to conservation efforts, they were reintroduced as the apex predator in 1995. This caused what is known as a trophic cascade. This is an ecological phenomenon that happens when an apex predator is removed from or introduced to an ecosystem. From top to bottom, the Yellowstone ecosystem was impacted by the reintroduction of the wolves.

4. Sustainable Human. "How Wolves Change Rivers".

The presence of the wolves, even when their numbers were small, caused behavioral changes in the deer and elk in that region. Their populations had been unchecked by the wolves for years which had caused overgrazing. But the deer began to expose themselves less in the open plains and near the water sources where they knew they were in more danger from the wolf packs. This caused changes in the open areas.

The grass and shrubs began regenerating and coming back stronger. As well, young trees had a better chance of growing with less pressure from the grazers and the open areas decreased. With the increase in trees, there was more room for various types of birds. The increase in trees also attracted an increasing number of beavers.

The beavers did what they are famous for—building dams. These dams created habitats for many creatures including fish, muskrats, and ducks. This, in turn, increased the biodiversity and health of the ecosystem.

During the absence of the wolves, coyotes had become the usurpers to their throne, a role for which they are not well-suited. Being smaller than wolves and generally not running in packs, the coyotes are much less capable of hunting the larger game such as deer or elk. Coyotes mainly prey on smaller animals such as mice and rabbits.

When the wolves came back, they pushed out this competitor, lowering the number of coyotes in the area. This too caused an increase in biodiversity because the numbers of the smaller prey creatures then began to increase. This meant that there was more food for a variety of other smaller predators such as foxes, hawks, and eagles.

The predation of the wolf packs created more carcasses. This gave increased opportunity to buzzards and ravens to clean up the leftovers. Even bears, another semi-competitor of wolves, benefited from their presence. The upsurge in scrubs and bushes meant more berries and the healthier bear population also helped in controlling the deer and elk.

But perhaps the most amazing change was seen in the rivers. You see, with the decrease in grazing, there were more plants near the riverbanks making them less likely to erode. This stabilized the banks and better held the rivers on their course. As they became more fixed in their course, they cut more deeply down instead of becoming wider. A deeper river is also more biodiverse, giving opportunities to more aquatic life. This also increased the Yellowstone area's drought resistance with a more stable supply of water.

So, wolves can change rivers. And, this story is not just for naturalists. It is another dramatic example of God's relationality. He created ecosystems where everything is reliant on everything else. This balance is at the core of life here on earth. He is sending a very clear message through interconnectedness; relationships are of great importance to him.

Social Interactions

A Mind Behind the Behavior

Before I begin this chapter, I want to apologize, because there are going to be many sentences in this chapter that end in question marks. That's not normally the way most people would write a book, and some might find it frustrating. But as I began to write this chapter, I realized it was going to involve lots of pondering about the "whys" behind social interactions. And contemplation often involves meandering through questions as you look at different possibilities. I would rather present it as queries because I want you to ponder as well. Even as I write, I'm not sure where we might travel, but I do know where we will end up. So, come along as we explore more deeply some things you may take for granted about social behaviors and let's see where this leads us.

Scientists explain social behaviors as part of Darwin's survival of the fittest. This theory contends that the behavior of living creatures can be traced back to an urge to survive and outcompete other creatures. Therefore, any creature that does not survive was simply unfit.[1]

Scientists do this because of a lack of other explanations within nature to account for these behaviors. My job will be to show you that this theory cannot possibly be the only force at work. Yes, survival is of central importance but when you start digging, it cannot describe everything that we see in social behavior nor the

1. Dictionary.com, "Survival of the Fittest".

impulses behind it. Animals and humans display interactions that are not so easily characterized.

We have looked at categorical relationships and the interconnectedness of life, but the highest form of relationality is social behavior. Why? Because the more intelligence is associated with an animal, the more likely it is to be highly social. This holds true with animals such as dolphins, elephants and apes—all of which are highly social and highly intelligent.

We humans seem to be attracted to the higher forms of life because we are fascinated by their social behavior. Probably because it echoes our own. Don't believe me? Post a video of a cute kitten playing with the family dog and then one of snails sitting on a leaf. See which one gets the most views, likes and comments of, "Aw, that is so cute!" Or, go to a zoo and check out how most people will watch the amusing antics of the monkeys but skip the insect exhibit.

Most of the time, intelligence and social behavior go together. But there are exceptions. Ants are not particularly smart creatures. They have tiny heads and even smaller brains, but in one way their social behavior is off the charts. I will call this hyper-social behavior "group-think." They rarely seem to think of themselves, opting instead to simply perform the role they have within the colony.

Ants, along with other social insects such as bees and wasps, appear to have little to no sense of self. Not unlike the fantasy Borg civilization found in some Star Trek episodes, each ant behaves as one part of the bigger collective. Everything they do is for their colony and queen, and their loyalty is absolute. The colony works almost as a single organism to provide everything they need for the success of the group.

This group-think is absolute to the point of ants giving up every active moment and their very lives for the good of the colony. Interestingly, even the queen is subject to it. When she is no longer useful to the colony, she will be immediately cast aside and even killed to make room for the new queen.

There are many interesting examples of ant group-think but, one of the best is seen in fire ants. As I have already explained, I live in Texas. A few decades ago, fire ants invaded. Now, it is impossible to go anywhere in east Texas without running into them. They are famous for furiously protecting their mounds, streaming out in all directions when the colony is disturbed. I can tell you from first-hand experience, they pack quite the sting. They are the pit-bulls of the ant world, grabbing hold with strong mandibles and not letting go.

Fire ants thrive in wet areas and when it gets too wet, they have an amazing survival strategy. When a colony is flooded, they form living rafts to make it to dry ground.[2] The worker ants make up the bottom of the raft, interlocking their water-repellent bodies to protect the queen and larvae above them. When they are interlocked, they make an amazingly strong and virtually unsinkable raft. Of course, these workers also risk death by getting separated, swept away or eaten by fish as they cross a river or pond. Undeterred, the colony floats to dry ground and relocates.

This appears to be a great example of survival of the fittest and, in many ways, it is. But let's zoom in on this behavior for a moment and ask some questions. As I have said, ants have tiny brains. How did they figure out this strategy? The first time an ant colony was ever flooded, did all the ants start screaming, "Everyone work together! We can make it if we create a raft from the bodies of the workers and float to safety!" How did the worker ants feel about being elected for this duty? Were there some who were like, "Hey, that seems like the short end of the stick. Why should I be at the bottom of the ship?"

Of course, this is silly but how do we come up with a better explanation? For this behavior to work, the ants of the first colony to exhibit this behavior had to decide at once, as a group, just as they were flooded to make the raft happen and save the colony. If they didn't get it right, there would be no second chances to "work out the kinks" and be more successful at this behavior the next time as the colony would be washed away and destroyed. Yet, somehow, it happened.

2. Nationalgeographic.com, "Fire Ants Make Living Raft."

This must have somehow happened as a result of group-think. But, where does that come from? Evolution could suggest there was a time when ants were much more independent thinkers, but those ants kept dying off until only group-thinkers remained because it was a better survival strategy for the ants. Seems far-fetched since group-think is a main factor in the survival of the colony, but let's go with that. When only group-thinkers remained, how did they work out the raft? That level of organization is extraordinary.

For humans to organize things, it takes lots of time in committees—discussing, debating, asking questions, getting direction, and making revisions. After all that, who knows if our plans will work? Can ants (or any animals for that matter) do any of that? Do they even have the ability to ask a question?

I think science would say that there isn't any thinking going on, the ants are just acting on instinct. Ok, fine. It's more fun to consider it the other way, but huge questions remain. To simply file all this amazing behavior under the category of "instincts" and leave it at that seems like painting with a very broad brush. Where did the raft instinct come from? For that matter, why is there such a thing as instinct? Could it be that science uses instincts to vaguely explain things that are otherwise unexplainable?

Another way science writes off difficult to explain behavior is to invoke an animal's will-to-live. Apparently, all animals become very creative in finding ways to keep from dying. It's believable to a certain extent. You can see it in examples like how a gazelle attempts to flee from a cheetah or a warthog furiously fighting off a hyena. But this sort of "will" is an individual thing and could even be thought of as selfish. Ants don't do selfish. So, is there such a thing as "group-will-to-live" for them? If so, where did that come from?

At the risk of over-beating the same drum, where does any will-to-live come from? We take it as a given that it exists, and for good reason. I certainly don't want to die. But, where does this urge come from? Do animals, especially the lower forms, understand life and death to the point of wanting to struggle to stay alive?

Does it work the same even for plants? They are extremely successful forms of life spreading everywhere across the earth. They appear to compete with one another for fertile soil and sunlight. But, can this be attributed to a will-to-live? Can plants, not having brains, even have a will? To make sense of this using just the natural world and survival of the fittest seems impossible.

Let's leave our ant friends and the plant world they live in without answers for the moment while we look at another curious example. Not all social behavior is warm and fuzzy. Some of it is down-right rough.

Falling squarely into survival of the fittest, lion social behavior revolves around the strongest male having rule over the pride.[3] But, when the alpha male grows old or weak, there is always a younger male lion nearby ready to take the job. Unfortunately, when this happens, infanticide is sure to follow. The new lion in charge, in an apparent bid to put the lionesses into heat again so he can pass on his genes, will begin killing off all the cubs of his predecessor. This grizzly affair happens regularly with the passing of the guard. It sounds straightforward enough and simply explained by Darwin's tenet. But is there more to it?

Consider what the lion must be aware of for this to happen. First, the new lion king needs to understand the consequences of lion copulation. Does he have the reasoning capacity to be able to put together sex and the babies that come from this union? Next, he will need to comprehend which offspring to kill and not kill. The adolescent lionesses are also his predecessor's daughters, but they will soon be of breeding age. Also, he must somehow understand that the soon to come new cubs will be his bloodline, so he will not kill them off in turn.

As well, he will have to somehow have the self-insight to understand and care about his own genealogy and legacy. The new alpha male would need to think to himself, "I'm certainly a prime example of a lion. I won the battle. Therefore, I should be the one to sire the next generation. As well, for some reason, I am really

3. Team Africa Geographic, "Understanding Lion Infanticide," paras. 1–2.

concerned about future generations. Even though I will be dead soon enough, I must pass on to them the very best."

As wise as the lion would need to be to think all this, science regularly passes it off as the explanation for why this infanticide, as well as so many other animal behaviors, happens. Apparently, all of nature is so concerned about the preservation and health of their species that this is their main goal in life. Even with the implications of very high intelligence in this theory, science simply takes it as a given and places it under the heading of instincts.

I have only presented three examples, but I would contend that there are more unexplainable behaviors in nature than there are species on earth. All creatures are fascinating and complex and exhibit amazing behaviors that lead to their success. How did caterpillars figure out how to morph into butterflies? How did the weaver birds figure out how to create such intricate nests? What caused the first dung beetle to roll dung? How did bees learn to find and gather nectar?

I would say these behaviors, when closely examined, are impossible to categorize under the headings of "they just figured it out themselves" or "instincts." Don't believe me? Then I would suggest you do some research yourself. But you will need to get past the surface and ask the hard questions. Apply your mind and heart and see what you discover. Decide whether you end up happy simply placing all these behaviors under the broad and somewhat mysterious category of "instincts" when you are done. For me, it just does not add up.

In a fascinating twist, naturalists seem to have some doubts as well. To fill the gap, they end up anthropomorphizing the laws of nature by saying, "It's all a part of Mother Nature's design." Seriously, who is Mother Nature? I cannot tell you how many wildlife shows have used that, or a similar phrase to neatly package up the whole of natural behavior. In the end, they have made nature into a sort of god and assign miraculous powers to it for a viable answer to why instincts exist. Ironically, they are actually getting closer to the truth.

Of course, there is an answer. What could organize all of nature to the most minuscule detail, make it highly interactive, give it a will-to-live, and an ultimate genealogical goal to keep it healthy and thriving? Sorry, I phrased that last sentence wrong because it could not be a "what." It must be a "who," because a "who" has the mind necessary to do this. And, there is only one "who" that has the capacity and power to achieve all this, our relational God.

In this immensely complex world teeming with life, God shows up in a big way. Each one of his creatures is carefully designed to have a particular role to fill and amazing behaviors that enable these creatures to thrive. He then uses social interactions to knit them together with these behaviors becoming more intimate, insightful, and even caring with the intelligence level of the creature. These behaviors move beyond simple survival into curiosity, playfulness, and deep family bonds. It just makes sense that all this must reflect what is important to their creator.

My argument above works fine for nature because the need for a mind is so obvious. But, what about humankind? We each already have an advanced mind. We can investigate profound things and make some sense of them and understand the consequences. So how does God's relationally show up in us? Through morality.

Morals are one of the things that separate us from the rest of life on earth. Except perhaps in the most rudimentary way, nature does not have morals. In fact, animals don't need morals. Crocodiles ambushing swimming wildebeests may seem wrong to us and a loyal golden retriever staying next to her sick owner may seem good, but we are just projecting our sense of morality onto the animals. These behaviors have no moral bearing because the animals are simply doing what they were created to do, following the instincts God has given them.

Humans, on the other hand, have more than just instincts. We have a conscience; a moral compass. From this conscience we gain values that make up a moral code. These codes are then used to create laws to hold people accountable for their actions. Not all human moral codes have been identical but, when you look at the roots of our morality across different cultures, they have striking similarities. By and large, we know right from wrong. When we act inappropriately, we know it. When we act altruistically, it is obvious. Only of mankind can it be said that we understand and exhibit good and evil.

If before I said that social behavior is the highest form of interactions, then morality is the highest form of social behavior. It is God working through us to show we are set apart and that he has a higher standard and purpose for us. The Bible calls this being made in God's image[4] and it is passionately relational. We will explore this further in the coming chapters.

So, from the categories found in the order of creation to the morality of humanity, relationality permeates God's creation. But this only accounts for the general revelation God has given about himself in his creation. Is there a special revelation about God recorded anywhere? Has God himself spoken to us about who he is? Does it support the idea that God is relational? In the next section, we will explore this possibility and its deep implications.

4. Gen 1:27, NIV.

SECTION THREE

Special Revelation

God in the Bible

Why the Bible?

A FEW YEARS AGO, I had a good friend come to me wanting to talk about a challenge he was having in his faith. My friend Dave is a solid, mature Christian who had already rode out some difficult times by staying close to Jesus. So, when he came to me, I knew he was not wavering over some insignificant detail.

We started a habit of walking together in the park next to my workplace. During these walks, we would struggle through this issue, talk about other important things, and pray for clarity. Dave's issue was the same one that I started this book with; the hiddenness of God. He did not understand why God, who showed himself in different ways so often in the Bible, seemed so distant and unavailable now. My friend felt frustration and even anger about why he didn't do this today.

We both talked about how grand it would be if God just burst out into the open and showed himself to everyone. He could do miracles, fix things, and speak wisdom to everyone until all doubt left that he truly exists. It would be so cool just to hang out with him and be his friend. We could share our difficulties with him and be calmed by his voice and sage advice. We could relate with him personally.

Does any of this make you yearn as well? Can you imagine what that would be like?

As we talked about these things, I certainly did not have all the answers, but I began to search. If I had been a deist relying on the general revelation found in creation, my search would have been short. Nature reveals precious little about why God chooses to remain hidden. I could see how this conundrum might cause a deist to slide the wrong direction on the Evolution of Faith. But I am not a deist, I am a Christian theist. I knew exactly where to find the answers. They were in the Bible. In learning about this issue and many other spiritual questions, the Bible did not disappoint.

Why the Bible? There are other options out there that purport to be scripture. Why not go with one of those? Great question. Let's investigate what makes the Bible so special.

From cover to cover, it is about God. It has been viewed by billions over the years to be the authority on God, his creation, and plan. As ancient as it is, it has survived and even thrived up to this day. It still captivates people and is the cause of great debate on exactly what it is. But there would be those who claim their scriptures do the same thing. What sets the Bible apart? One of the reasons dovetails into what I have already written about in this book.

What picture of God do scriptures outside the Bible paint? Is he a haughty emperor; a conquering general; a mysterious wizard; a wise but aloof sage? In them, how does God relate with his creation and humanity? Is he distant and cold? Does he care what happens to the world? Are we to grovel before him and simply do his bidding? How could we determine if this is what God is like?

Actually, we should already know if this would be an accurate picture because we have spent some time looking at God's character in his creation. God shows himself subtly, but when you begin to see him, he takes center stage. We have found that God is vastly powerful, orderly, meticulous, and has an amazing logical mind. We have also seen his heart in the beauty of his creation; how he cares enough to sustain it and make it flourish. His relationality shines through in how everything in the universe is categorical, interconnected, and interacting. Through his creation of us, we also know that he is social, loving, moral, and just—expecting the same from us.

Whatever religious texts we examine, we must find these characteristics as well. If we do not find them, that scripture is not giving a complete picture. Worse yet, that scripture may give conflicting characteristics from what God has already revealed in his creation. It is incongruent to believe contradictory things about God. God is not both cruel and caring, orderly and chaotic, or powerful and needy.

As I hope to show you in this final section, the Bible displays all the characteristics of God shown in creation in abundance. It is therefore completely consistent with general revelation. But it also goes so much deeper into who God is and further defines his relationality and our relationship to him.

The Bible is purported to be God's word, as if he wrote it *through* the many authors of its books. Christian theologians and adherents proclaim that it is therefore inerrant and without flaw. Sentiments on this abound. Could this document, written thousands of years ago, be the same as the copies we have today? In all its translations, does it hold on to the truth of the original authors? Could it possibly be relevant to our modern culture? Are there contradictions and fallacies?

What exactly is this book and how are we supposed to take it? Even as I fell in love with the Bible as a young Christian, I struggled with this often myself. But as I struggled, I became more and more confident that God was speaking to me through its pages. I grew in my belief that it is thoroughly reliable and relevant.

I am not a biblical scholar. I have not studied the original languages, nor have I done archeological digs in the Middle East. So, I needed a way to see the Bible that I could wrap my head around without getting lost in the theological details. I needed a practical approach that I could apply to my life. With this in mind, I came up with a definition of the Bible that has served me well since then and set many questions to rest. A description in which I have the highest confidence.

You see, the proof is in the pudding. Although it has been around for thousands of years, the Bible still piercingly addresses moral and spiritual issues and, although it has been greatly maligned, it continues to positively transform the lives of those who place their faith in the truths found within. No matter what language or part of the world you find it in, any honest translation does this. When looked at with an open heart to God's guidance, these scriptures have the power to change us. You may be skeptical of this, but I am certain for the simple reason that it has changed me in profound ways. Millions of other Christian would give the same testimony.

Therefore, I believe the Bible is from God and my description of it is simple; *the Bible does exactly what God intended it to do.* No matter what else you want to say about it, his document serves his purposes. As simple as this sentiment is, it is also profound. This means the Bible must be a living document that has not grown stale with age. It means that it is an agent of God that contains timeless truths that have the power to transform. What are God's purposes for the Bible?

Expose your heart and mind to it and it will enlighten your understanding of reality. It will challenge you with God's expectations and surprise you with his considerations. It will use the light of truth to tear down strongholds of lies in your life. It will force you to contend with your own shortcomings while encouraging you to see who you were truly created to be. It will perplex you through prophecies-yet-to-come and prove itself through prophecies fulfilled. It can be frightening yet show you there is no reason to fear. It will teach you to be wise while humbling you through its insights. It will counter the adversity in life and strengthen you to walk through it. It will shine the light of hope and teach you the true meaning of love. It will show you God's heart as it touches yours.

All these things God wants to share with you and more. It is all a part of his purpose for the Bible. He gave us an amazing document to open our eyes to all the things that the florescent lights of this concrete world make hard to see.

Perhaps you want proof of what I am claiming about the Bible. I could spend some time doing just that but there is a better way for you to find this proof: read it yourself. Just remember to read it *with* God.

Instead, my aim is to show God's relationality through the pages of the Bible. Come along as we open them and dive into his true nature.

The Name of the Living God

The Bible has such an embarrassment of riches when it comes to God's relationality that I found it very difficult to whittle down what I would focus on. I could have described how he associated with Abraham, Isaac, and Joseph through whom he created the lineage of his chosen people. I could have talked about how God delivered the Israelites from Egypt and personally led them through the desert to the promised land. I could also have focused on the prophets and shown how God used them as a direct line of communication to others, giving them his truth. I could have told you the story of King David and how he was a man after God's own heart.

All these things would have shown how God relates to us in a personal way. But, as I thought and prayed through this process, my focus began to narrow. The subjects started to float to the top and be organized into a story. And, a story should begin with a proper introduction. The first thing you learn about a person when you meet them is their name. So, let me introduce you to the God of the Bible by telling you his.

In the book of Exodus, God shows himself to Moses in the form of a burning bush. When Moses inquires about God's name, he says:

> *"I AM WHO I AM. This is what you are to say to the Israelites: 'I AM has sent me to you.'" —Exod 3:14*

The literal translation of this name from the Hebrew is YHWH. It is impossible to pronounce without vowels, so when they are added, YHWH takes on two forms, Yahweh or Jehovah. The Jewish people believed this name to be so holy that they would not utter or write it. Instead, in most Bible translations, you will find the word LORD in all caps to signify Yahweh and to differentiate it from Adonai, another word meaning Lord often used in reference to God.

The name of God is profound, mysterious, and deep. But of course, it would be. A name fit for God must be more than just a moniker. "Bob," "Frank," or "George" isn't going to cut it. God's name is much more because it is a remarkable description of his deity.

There are many implications wrapped up in his name; far too many to attempt to unravel here. But the fact of his *actuality* and position of *pre-eminence* are clearly seen at the forefront.

First, God says, "I AM." God is—he *actually* is. Although there might be doubters, his status is not in doubt. Moses certainly had no uncertainty. God's existence, presence, and work were powerfully and undeniably before him. For God to announce "I AM" also infers that all his attributes are real as well. I can testify to the fact that when one begins to grasp the truths about his characteristics, it is an overwhelming reality that the only correct response to is worship.

Then God says, "WHO I AM." Because there are none to compare to him, God simply references himself as a descriptor. To do anything less would not be fitting. This strange sounding statement ends up making perfect sense because there is nothing else he could have likened himself to without falling short of his status and his name.

In this passage, God chose to reveal this personal information to Moses. Moreover, since it is recorded in scripture, God has allowed humanity to know as well. He certainly didn't have to. He could have been vague. He could have sent a messenger in his stead. He could have remained silent. But he didn't. He revealed his distinct name. By telling us this, Yahweh is indicating that he is personal and willing to be intimately known.

This passage also demonstrates that he is accessible. He broke into Moses' world in a big way. Although we may not all encounter a burning bush, accessibility can come in different forms. We too can encounter God in a personal way. How might this happen?

The Bible gives us insight into this as well. In many verses it proclaims that God is near. For example, it states:

> *"The LORD is near to all who call on him, to all who call on him in truth."* —*Ps 145:18*

Pretty obvious, isn't it? God is near and accessible "*to all who call on him.*" He generally does not force himself on people, but he is there. That would also suggest that he tends to remain hidden to those who do not call on him. The principle appears to be—Want to see him? Call on him in truth and he will draw near. Don't want to see him? Don't call on him and he will remain hidden. The Bible says more to clarify this which we will delve into later. But for now, please note there is a choice for us to make.

Yahweh is God's name, but throughout scripture, we see descriptors or titles added to his name to further clarify who he is. Some of them describe his power and majesty, but many directly describe his relationality. Let's look at a few of them.

Yahweh Jireh means The Lord Will Provide.[1] This name for God is found in Genesis where the patriarch Abraham is tested by God. God tells Abraham to sacrifice his son Isaac as an offering to him. Abraham dutifully sets out to do this but, just as he is about to plunge the knife into Isaac, God stops him.

> *"Do not lay a hand on the boy," he said. "Do not do anything to him. Now I know that you fear God, because you have not withheld from me your son, your only son."*
> —*Gen 22:12*

Instead, God provides a ram to be sacrificed. So, Abraham calls the place where the sacrifice was to take place Yahweh Jireh.[2]

Indeed, The Lord has provided us with an abundantly fruitful planet that can satisfy the needs of over seven billion people. When someone provides you with a meal, it is a caring gift. Ultimately,

1. Piper, "Jehovah Jireh," para. 3.
2. Gen 22:14, NIV.

every meal and every other form of provision comes from God. Need air? The atmosphere is full of it. Need sight? He gave us a pair of eyes. Need knowledge? He has given us a brain. Need companionship? He has surrounded us with people to choose from. I could go on, but you get the point. He cares for us enough to provide for all our needs. As we will soon see, God has provided not only for our physical needs but for our spiritual needs as well.

Yahweh Rapha means The Lord Who Heals.[3] This name for God is found in several places in the Bible including Jeremiah, Isaiah, and the Psalms.

> *Praise the Lord, my soul, and forget not all his benefits—*
> *who forgives all your sins and heals all your diseases . . .*
> *—Ps 103:2–3*

You would not be wrong to think of a doctor when you consider this. But you should also think of the loving comfort of a mother as she puts a band-aid on her child's knee. Consider also that your body is an amazing healing machine without which we would not be able to survive. Along with physical healing, we heal emotionally, psychologically, and, most importantly, spiritually. It is this spiritual healing that God ultimately wants to give us.

Yahweh Shalom means The Lord is Peace.[4] The story surrounding this name of God is found in the book of Judges, chapter 6. A man named Gideon had been chosen by God to save Israel from being oppressed by a group called the Midianites. Gideon was unconvinced that he was the man for the job, so he sought reassurance that God was truly with him. He did this by putting out an offering of bread and meat for God to see what would happen. God himself came in the form of an angel and miraculously consumed the offering.

Rather than reassure Gideon, this terrified him because he knew no one could see the holiness of God and survive. However,

3. Kalu, "What Does it Mean That God is Jehova-Rapha?," para. 1.

4. Ryan, "What Does it Mean That God is Jehovah-Shalom?" para. 1.

God told Gideon to be at peace because nothing would happen to him. So, Gideon called the place of the offering Yahweh Shalom.[5]

The word Shalom means more than the absence of conflict. It is a picture of everything being in a state of harmony. Imagine everything in your life working perfectly. No conflict or frustration. No difficulties or sorrow. No lost opportunities or regrets. Even though we can never find this level of peace in this world, being in relationship with the God of peace gives us a taste of what this would be like in Heaven.

Some of God's titles begin with word El, which denotes power and might.[6] But one such name is strikingly personal and warm. The name *El Roi* means the God Who Sees Me.[7] Yes, it means that God is all-seeing, but there is more to it than that. In the book of Genesis, chapter 16, we see the story of Hagar and her son Ishmael fleeing from Abraham's wife Sarah. Hagar was being mis-treated by Sarah because she was jealous of the son Hagar had borne to Sarah's husband Abraham. God finds Hagar in the desert and tells her to go back to Abraham's encampment and he will bless her. At this Hagar says,

> *You are the God who sees me . . . I have now seen the one who sees me. —Gen 16:13*

Hagar was a simple servant girl. She was used to being overlooked. She was astounded that the God of the universe cared enough to come find her and *acknowledge* her. He didn't ignore her; he didn't look past her; he saw her and spoke blessing into her life. This speaks of God's tenderness and concern for people whom others might consider insignificant.

One more name that should be included in my list is directly attributed to Jesus in the new testament. It is *Immanuel.* In the book of Matthew, the story of the birth of Jesus is being described. It says:

5. Judg 6:24, NIV.
6. Parsons, "The Hebrew Names for God—El," para. 1.
7. Parsons, "The Hebrew Names for God—El," para. 12.

> *All this took place to fulfill what the Lord had said through the prophet: "The virgin will conceive and give birth to a son, and they will call him Immanuel"—which means "God with us." —Matt 1:22–23*

The implications are far ranging, but let's just focus on the idea of God being *with* us. Jesus was literally with humanity during his time on earth and part of his mission was to portray God to us in a way the world had never seen before. In Christ, God came down to intermingle with humanity and show his heart to us all.

Provision, healing, peacefulness, acknowledgement, and interaction with us—all these characteristics are highly relational. God is clearly demonstrating to us through these titles how important this is to him. It surely is not a stretch to call him our relational God.

Allow me to cut in here and make an important clarifying point. To interact with us, God must be alive. Obvious, right? You can't socialize with an inanimate object or dead person. If he is the author of all life, as I have already argued, he must be alive.

In contrast, the Old Testament speaks about idols. The Bible tells us that an idol is a false god. In the book of Isaiah chapter 44, there is a section addressing the foolishness of idol worship. Take a moment yourself and read verses twelve through twenty. In that section, a man carves an idol out of a half-used piece of firewood and then bows down to worship it. The wood is dead and the idol behind it is false, but the man still prostrates himself before it. This is an affront to the true God. Yahweh is real and alive while those idols are phony, powerless, and lifeless. The lesson is, don't be fooled by a fake that has no ability to relate to you.

Through his names we see a God who is personal. He is alive and active. He is near and accessible. In the form of his son Jesus, he even came to visit us. His names are more than just names; they are expressions of who he is. Now that we know God's name, let's begin to look at his nature.

The Three in One

To UNDERSTAND GOD'S NATURE, you must examine the Trinity. This is a theological term that describes the mystery of God being three in one. He is the Father, the Son, and the Holy Spirit. Yet, he is one. He is three persons that are one essence. I know this is difficult to comprehend. In our world, this would be impossible. But we are talking about an all-powerful God who is spirit, not material. And, this is how he has presented himself to us.

My aim in this book is not to explain the Trinity, just to present it and show his relationality through it. If you would like to delve into the topic of the Trinity, The Bible Project has put out a very good video simply titled, "God."[1] I recommend you check it out. One observation I will make is that the Trinity is the zenith of relationality. In the flawless oneness of the three, God is literally the perfect relationship!

The first person of the Trinity is the Father. When you consider God, this is likely how you think of him. For me, the term father just seems to intrinsically fit God. The biblical scripture sets itself apart from other religious texts by giving a strong, clear picture of God as a father. Not only in name, but in character.

In one sense, as our creator, the word father fits because God gave us all life. So yes, we are all God's children in this way. But the Bible moves well beyond this, and as you will see later, God's fatherhood takes on greater meaning when it comes to salvation.

1. Bible Project, "God."

Sometimes people will have difficulty with the thought of God as our father. This can happen when that person's fatherly examples are poor ones. In a world where there are plenty of absent, selfish, cruel, or deadbeat dads, the thought of God as a father may not be a positive one. It can cause one to be fearful or angry at this imagery of God.

But none of those negative terms fit God. Instead, all the characteristics we need in a good dad should come to mind. God the Father is strong but kind, firm but fair. He is our ultimate source of protection and provision. He teaches and challenges us. He disciplines his children so that we will grow and mature, but it is all done with the deepest love. He cares about our well-being and wants the best for us. He is the father that we all yearn for; the one we would want to make proud.

Here are some great verses that describe God the Father:

> *A Father to the fatherless, a defender of widows, is God in his holy dwelling. God sets the lonely in families, he leads forth the prisoners with singing —Ps 68:5–6*
>
> *"Your Father knows what you need before you ask him." —Matt 6:8*
>
> *He shielded him and cared for him; he guarded him as the apple of his eye . . . —Deut 32:10*
>
> *Your Father in heaven is not willing that any one of these little ones should be lost. —Matt 18:14*
>
> *For this reason I kneel before the Father, from whom every family in heaven and on earth derives its name. —Eph 3:14–15*

Are you getting the picture? God, as described in the Bible, is the perfect example of fatherhood. He does not want to simply be our creator. He wants the rich, loving relationship of a father to his children. If you consider the fact that he created the family, which is the basic unit of all humanity, of course he does! Later, we will discuss what it means to become a child of God, but for now, soak in the reassuring image of who he ultimately wants to be for us.

As wonderful as that image is, this is only the first way God presents himself to us. There are two other persons of the Trinity. The second is as the Son, Jesus Christ.

Interestingly, when Jesus spoke to his father, he used a term of endearment and familiarity. Jesus called God "Abba." This would be much like you or I using the term "Daddy." It is this intimacy that he wanted to demonstrate to us as something we could choose to have with God.[2] For us, this should conjure up imagery of a small child being picked up into her father's strong arms and held close.

Jesus is our most concrete example of God's relationality. He plainly showed us exactly how God relates during the time he was here on earth. So, what did Jesus do while he was here? Did he hide away in a dark cave? Did he speak condescendingly down to everyone from on high? Did he make his disciples into bodyguards, forcing everyone to keep their distance? Did he fry people with a bolt of lightning if they dare question his authority?

Of course not. As he is presented in the Gospels, he is kind, gentle, giving, and caring—allowing anyone to come to him. Let's look at some verses that back this up:

> *When he saw the crowds, he had compassion on them, because they were harassed and helpless, like sheep without a shepherd. —Matt 9:36*
>
> *"Come to me, all you who are weary and burdened, and I will give you rest. Take my yoke upon you and learn from me, for I am gentle and humble in heart, and you will find rest for your souls. For my yoke is easy and my burden is light." —Matt 11:28–30*
>
> *He tends his flock like a shepherd: He gathers the lambs in his arms and carries them close to his heart; he gently leads those that have young. —Isa 40:11*
>
> *When Jesus landed and saw a large crowd, he had compassion on them and healed their sick. —Matt 14:14*

2. Bernock, "What Does it Mean That God is Our Abba Father?," para.14.

Jesus was undeniably compassionate and relational. This can also be seen in how he treated his disciples and how he taught them. He was not like a professor at the front of a class spewing out facts for one hour each school day. No, he intimately shared his life with them. They went everywhere as a group. They ate, drank, slept, and traveled together. They laughed, cried, and experienced life together. All the while he would pour into them the spiritual truths that changed them from fishermen and tax collectors into men who would soon carry the message that would change the world.

He made himself so accessible to everyone that he had no time to himself unless he snuck away at night to be alone with his father or took a nap in the bottom of the boat in which they were traveling. As well, he went *to* the people. He did not sit on a throne and force everyone to travel miles to see his miracles, he moved from place to place to be available. During his ministry; Jesus did not have a home. He and the disciples were nomadic, searching out people to touch with his love and wisdom.

There is an amazing passage in the book of Hebrews that shows how deeply relational Christ's mission was. Read the second chapter of Hebrews from verse nine through verse eighteen and you will get the fuller picture. You see, Jesus took on flesh and blood so that he could *share* in our humanity. He was made like us in every way to experience the trials of being human. He suffered and was tempted as a human to empathize with us fully as our savior. He did not spare himself anything.

You have heard it said that a great leader is willing to go into battle with his troops. But, this pales in comparison to what Christ did in his humanity. He showed how deeply he loved us by setting aside many of the trappings of his godhead to walk in our shoes. He came down from heaven and subjected himself to the difficulties of mortal life and the pain of death.

That is why the Bible can truthfully proclaim:

> *In your relationships with one another, have the same mindset as Christ Jesus: Who being in very nature god, did not consider equality with God something to be used to his own advantage; rather, he made himself nothing*

> *by taking the very nature of a servant, being made in human likeness. And being found in appearance as a man, he humbled himself by becoming obedient to death—even death on a cross! —Phil 2:5–8*

Having considered the Son, you might think that there is no better example of God's relationality. But there is one more member of the Trinity.

The Holy Spirit is sometimes referred to as the most quiet and mysterious person of the Trinity. He is quiet in that one of his roles is to remind us of the things that Jesus and the Father have said instead of speaking distinctly for himself. He never pushes himself forward. Although he is fully God, he chooses to be subordinate to the Father and Son, just as Jesus chooses to be subordinate to the Father.

He is mysterious in the way he works. Jesus describes him as being like the wind, going where he pleases. You don't see him coming and you don't know where he goes. He is likened to the breath of God. In fact, the same word used for wind and breath in the Bible, *ruach*, can also mean Spirit.[3] Because of this, some people have mistakenly seen the Holy Spirit as simply a mindless force. But the Bible shows that he has full personhood.

Jesus himself is one of our main sources of information about the Holy Spirit. In the gospel of John, Jesus speaks of him extensively. Check out chapters 3, 14, and 16 and you will see all the things that Jesus said about him. The Holy Spirit is seen in his personhood when Jesus calls him the Counselor or Advocate. Being a counselor would be impossible for anything less than a person.

This is where we begin to see his relationality. Think about what a counselor does. They are trained to give guidance on personal, social, or psychological issues. They are there to help us work through life's challenges and point us in the right direction. The Holy Spirit does all this as well as giving the most important type of counsel—spiritual. He is the one who will guide us towards all the right choices concerning God, morality, and spirituality.

3. Schultz, "Spirit Definition," paras. 1–3.

How does this work? In explaining about the Holy Spirit, Jesus said to his disciples:

> *. . . But you know him, for he lives with you and will be in you. —John 14:17*

First, Jesus said, "*he lives with you.*" This is very similar to the concept we looked at earlier of God being near and accessible to those who call on him. Just reach out and he is there. Second, Jesus said, "*and will be in you.*" What does that mean? It is speaking of being indwelt. This is a term used to describe the Holy Spirit's relation to a given person. He either deals with us "outside-in" or "inside-out."

The outside-in working of the Holy Spirit is his dealings with a non-believer. He can touch that person's heart with experiences and insights that lead him or her toward the right choices. He will also convict them of sinful behavior or show them a better way. This is not forcing; it is being an outside influence. You have probably experienced it yourself. When your conscience was unexpectedly pricked over something hurtful you did or a wrong attitude you held, this can be the work of the Holy Spirit. You briefly encounter him and then he is gone like the wind. He draws near and touches you but then moves on.

The inside-out working of the Holy Spirit is reserved for believers. When a person receives Christ through the truth of the Gospel, the Bible teaches we are literally indwelt by the Holy Spirit. His presence comes to abide inside our spirit in an amazing unity. The Bible says in Ephesians that believers are "sealed" with the Holy Spirit, suggesting that this is a permanent change.

This is part of what it means to become a "new person" in Christ.[4] Believers have the Spirit of God dwelling permanently inside so that the Spirit can be with them though all their experiences in life. The Holy Spirit is now a continual influence and a believer can tap into him any time for help with anything. When a believer follows his guidance, it is called the out-working of the Holy Spirit in their life. Quite the upgrade!

4. 2 Cor 5:17, NIV.

Think about this in relational terms. A believer is so close to God that he or she literally has God within! Talk about getting to the heart of the matter. You can't get more intimate than that! I hope at this point you are asking, "So how does a person become indwelt by the Holy Spirit?" This is a great question that I will be tackling in the last section of this book. So, read on!

Whether in the person of the Father, Son, or Holy Spirit, God shows us a personality that shines brightly with relationality. But even this is only a fraction of who God is. Let's look at some more of God's characteristics to get a fuller view.

A More Complete Picture

Not surprisingly in a book titled Our Relational God, I have devoted the greatest portion of it to describing this one characteristic of God. Obviously, God has many other amazing attributes including those that only God could have. Yahweh is all-seeing, all-knowing, all-powerful, and eternal. He is also unchanging, infinite, and beyond our ability to fully comprehend.

The danger of bringing forward one characteristic over all the others is to give an unbalanced view of God. At this point, because of my emphasis, some of my readers may think of God as one big cuddly teddy bear. Or they may see him as a grandfatherly type who would never hold us to any standard. Even worse, they could think of him as desperate for attention, practically begging us to like him. But this would be a serious mistake. These images are just as idolatrous as the person who thinks God is a genie in a bottle, waiting to do their bidding.

Therefore, it is important that I touch on some of his qualities that could be deemed non-relational. These characteristics could be thought of as God's "otherness." It is how he is different than we are. Although these qualities will show the challenges to his relationality, they will also show us the proper boundaries that a relationship with Yahweh should have. Besides, "otherness" is a quality in everyone. You can't have a relationship without another. To only relate with yourself is a lonely, selfish thing. And, although we all have similarities, we are also each unique.

The Old Testament tells us in many places to fear God. This sounds like a relationship killer. Who can relate with a God that they are afraid of? But the proper understanding of this phrase is to stand in awe and give the highest respect to the creator of the universe. This is the correct attitude and perspective to have. Let's look at some of his awe-inspiring attributes and expand our understanding.

God's attributes overlap. To talk about one, you will often need to talk about others. This is true with God's holiness. In the book of Isaiah chapter 6, it tells of Isaiah first being in the presence of God. He describes a vision of God enthroned; high and exalted with angels surrounding him.

> *And they were calling to one another: "Holy, holy, holy is the LORD Almighty; the whole earth is full of his glory."* —*Isa 6:3*

Holiness can be defined as being set apart in absolute purity. God is perfectly holy. Even the angels in the vision covered their faces and were unable to look upon his countenance. Isaiah says in response to being in God's presence:

> *"'Woe to me!' I cried. 'I am ruined! For I am a man of unclean lips, and I live among a people of unclean lips, and my eyes have seen the King, the LORD Almighty.'"* —*Isa 6:5*

In his sinfulness, Isaiah knew he was unworthy to be in God's presence. God needed to provide him purification before sending Isaiah to be his prophet. God's holiness cannot be defiled by anything evil or impure. In fact, any place the presence of the Father touches drives out impurity and becomes holy itself. Earlier, we saw that Moses met God in the form of a burning bush in the book of Exodus. During this encounter, God tells Moses to remove his sandals because he is standing on holy ground.

We, like Isaiah and Moses, are not holy. On our own, we can never achieve this perfection. We are therefore not worthy to be in God's presence. This seems to be an insurmountable problem. How does a God of holiness relate with sinful people? Although we as fallen creatures cannot resolve this question, God has solved it for us in more than one way. The answer is multi-faceted and gets us into other aspects of who he is.

First, we need to understand the concept of veiling. Because we could never stand in the presence of the holy Father, he veils himself in different ways. Again, think back to God's encounter with Moses. Instead of overwhelming Moses with his presence, God comes in the form of a burning bush. He unmistakably presents himself, but in a way that Moses can handle. He also does this during the crossing of the red sea, showing himself to the Israelites as the Shekinah Glory. This pillar of cloud by day and fire by night was obviously God but did not overwhelm them.

Veiling is the reason that Jesus did not overwhelm people with his presence. Jesus was fully God, but he was also fully man.

> *For in Christ all the fullness of the Deity lives in bodily form . . . —Col 2:9*

His humanity veiled his godliness so that men could interact with him freely and without fear. This veiling was key to Jesus' ministry here on earth. It is how he could so personally relate with us. It is how he became Immanuel—God with us.

We also see this with the Holy Spirit. I am going to make the most obvious statement ever, but it is important. The Holy Spirit is holy and spirit. Just like God the Father and Son, he is holy, and we could not directly contact him in our unholiness. The reason he can interact with people is that in his spirit-ness, he is veiled to those in the material. But he can interact with individuals in spiritual ways. As we have already seen, in a believer, he interacts directly with our spirit through indwelling.

This brings up questions about the nature of the spiritual world. Without getting too heady, the spiritual world can be thought of as where God is, or Heaven. In contrast, we are in the material world and currently, the spiritual realm is in many ways veiled to us. This is by necessity because the spiritual would overwhelm the material if it were not. Here's why.

In the last two chapters of Revelation, we see a vision from the apostle John describing the end times and the Holy City. It is beautiful, so I encourage you to read it. It starts with this:

> *Then I saw a new heaven and a new earth, for the first heaven and the first earth had passed away, and there was no longer any sea. I saw the Holy City, the new Jerusalem, coming down out of heaven from God . . . —Rev 21:1–2*

To clarify, the "first heaven" referred to is the material cosmos; the stars we see in the sky at night. The "new heaven" and the "Holy City" are the spiritual Heaven. There are two things I want to point out regarding this.

First, the Holy City comes down to earth. You see, we do not go up to Heaven as most people think; it comes down to us. There is no stairway to Heaven. We could never ascend to it on our own, literally or figuratively, so God must bring it to us.

Second, the old, material earth passes away. Apparently, God needs to make it new. This can be interpreted as the earth being revitalized into something that is compatible with the spiritual realm although it may mean it is completely replaced with the spiritual. Either way, that is why the spiritual and the material are currently separated. When unveiled, the spiritual world will bring radical changes to this fallen, material world.

With this new information we can also circle back to the hiddenness of God. As frustrating as this can sometimes be, he is hidden to protect us in our material, fallen state. This is why he is the glow-in-the-dark God. He is unseen, but he wants us to know he is there. So, he enables us to sense him in orderliness, beauty, life, morality, and in our yearnings for eternity—for something more than meets the eye.

Although we must go quite a way to understand how God's holiness affects his relationality, it is worth the trip. With this understanding we can appreciate what he has done to reach down to us without compromising who he is. The term for this is condescension. It is God's voluntary descent from his high and exalted position to relate with us. We could never reach him so, in various ways, Yahweh has stretched out his hand to us.

Closely akin to God's holiness is his righteousness. This means that he is morally flawless and justified in everything he does. In fact, he is the absolute moral standard; the plumb line by which we can see when we have gone wrong.

This facet is also proof of God's existence because if there is an absolute moral standard that exists outside of us, then someone must have put it there. If there are some things that are always wrong and some things that are always right, then there is an ethical standard given to us by an ethical God.

God's righteousness leads to justice. This is because in his righteousness, God cannot leave wrongs unaccounted for. The Bible clearly tells us that there will be a day when all evil and unrighteousness will be judged and condemned.

> *For we know him who said, "It is mine to avenge; I will repay," and again, "The Lord will judge his people." It is a dreadful thing to fall into the hands of the living God.*
> *—Heb 10:30–31*

Of course, this strains the idea of him being relational, right? There are many people who say they could not believe in a God who is judgmental. They certainly can embrace God's love and kindness, but they are repelled by this idea that one day humankind will stand before our judge and may face condemnation. What if I were to tell you that this is exactly the kind of God you want?

You see, a righteous God is going to make everything right in the end. He will wipe clean everything evil and wrong that has ever happened. When God judges the world, there will be nothing left but goodness and love leading to perfect relationships where no one has anything to hold against anyone else.

Let me put it another way. If you do not want God to judge mankind, which of the unjust acts do you want him to keep? Which ones are okay for God to "look the other way" on? What about the wrongs committed against you? Are you fine with him leaving any of those unaccounted for? Or are you hoping he will judge the wickedness of others but not look at your own wrongdoings?

That's not the way it works. It's all or nothing. There will not be one evil deed left unaccounted for. He will not leave a speck of dirt in any corner. In your heart of hearts, you know this because God has planted in you a sense of justice as well, and that sense resonates with his righteousness.

We must remember that God is the *perfect* judge. He is not going to misjudge anything. It will all be taken care of in a way that will make everyone say, "Yep, that's the way it should have happened." And, when all that is evil and unrighteous is taken care of, what a wonderful place will be left! So, I say with the Bible:

> *. . . let justice roll on like a river, righteousness like a never-failing stream! —Amos 5:24*

So yes, God can be holy, righteous, and the bringer of justice and still be relational. He can set appropriate boundaries and have expectations of his creation and still be loving and caring. In fact, this is what makes him the perfect father. These characteristics are exactly what will bring about a perfect relationship in the end.

As you have been reading this chapter, at some point you may have thought, "But what about forgiveness? Are we all doomed? Surely a good and just God would show mercy and grace as well?"

That is the most exciting part! It is what God planned all along. You see, God's plan for all of humankind is, of course, crazy-level relational as well. Let's take a close look and see what he has in store.

SECTION FOUR

God's Relational Plan

Normal and Abnormal

Let me give you another reason to read the Bible. God's entire plan for his creation is outlined in it. Yep, that's right. If you want to know what he has done, what he is doing, and even what he is planning on doing, read the Bible. God isn't keeping his plan a secret from us, he lays it all out for anyone to see and invites us to discover it.

Most households in the United States have at least one Bible.[1] After all, we are called a Christian nation. Yet that book, which contains everything God wants you to know about him, sits up on a shelf somewhere collecting dust. Either we do nothing to learn more about God or we wait for pastors or priests to spoon feed us little morsels rather than seeing what God is all about for ourselves.

If anyone doesn't have a Bible, they can go to any bookstore and find a wide variety of translations to suit their taste and dive right in. It is the best-selling book in all of history by a wide margin. But, is it read as much as it is bought?

And you, dear reader . . . how about you? You picked up this book about God, but do you know what he has said in his own words? I can promise you, his book is much better than this one. In case you were wondering, yes, I am trying to make you feel a pang of guilt. Maybe you should. Our relational God wants to tell you all about himself and what he wants for you and you may be ignoring him.

1. Christian Research, "The Bible," para. 3.

I'll stop lecturing now because for nearly thirty years of my life I did the same thing. Growing up, I attended church, but as soon as I moved out for college, that was in my rearview mirror. I certainly did not read the Bible during this time because I was too busy being selfish, partying, and chasing after coeds. Perhaps you can relate. It was only after hitting some nasty bumps in my life that I began to see my need for a relationship with God and the wisdom found in his book. When I finally stopped ignoring him, my entire world changed for the better. I simply want the same for you.

I am going to assume that very few biblical scholars are reading this book. Since I am not a scholar either, I will try to present the Bible to you in a practical, applicable way. So, let me show you the big picture—the very big picture.

Not surprisingly, his plan all along was to bring us into relationship with him. How does he do that? It can be summed up by four words: *creation, fall, redemption*, and *restoration*. Let's consider each theme a little further and get a taste of what you might be missing.

The creation story is in the book of Genesis. Yes, there is much controversy over whether we should take the events that happen at the beginning literally, but let's set that aside for the moment. Instead, let's simply assume that God has something to teach us in the story of Adam and Eve and see what we learn.

At first, the story is zoomed out, showing Yahweh creating the universe. You see his creative energies hard at work as the world takes form and then explodes with life. God speaks, and it happens. He says, "Let there be . . ." and there it is. Light, water, sky, land, vegetation, trees, sun, moon, stars, fish, birds and land animals. All God had to do was utter the words and these things came into being. Then God said:

> *"Let us make mankind in our image, in our likeness, so that they may rule over the fish in the sea and the birds in the sky, over the livestock and all the wild animals, and over all the creatures that move along the ground." So God created*

> *mankind in his own image, in the image of God he created them; male and female he created them.* —Gen 1:26–27

Out of all his creation, mankind alone is made "*in his own image*." We have been set apart as image bearers of God. In chapter 2 the story zooms in and we learn more about how God created man.

> *Then the Lord God formed a man from the dust of the ground and breathed into his nostrils the breath of life, and the man became a living being.* —Gen 2:7

Notice that God didn't just speak man into existence as he had the rest of creation. Instead, he formed him and directly breathed life into him. Part of what God meant when he said we were made in his image is that we have the breath of God in us. We learned earlier that the Hebrew word for breath also means spirit. We have a spirit breathed directly into us from our creator.

But, what is this spirit? We see it in this passage, and I have talked about the spirit earlier, but how do you define it? Although the Bible uses this word differently in varying contexts, I will focus on the main aspect that is seen in the verse above. The Bible also says:

> *God is spirit, and his worshipers must worship in the Spirit and in truth.* —John 4:24

God made Adam special using his spirit to bring him to life. Some people mistakenly believe that being made in the image of God means we physically look like God. But, since God is spirit instead of flesh, that cannot be true. We are image bearers of God in that we have a spirit that is reflective of him, and when we worship, we commune with God in our spirit.

The nature of spirit is difficult to understand because there is little in a material universe with which to compare it. Perhaps the best example would be energy. In part, it is a powerful, animating, immaterial force that enables humans to interface with God. This spirit did not simply bring Adam to life, it also allowed him to interact with God in a special way above all of creation. Therefore, we can think of our spirit as that place inside us where we relate with God.

In much of the rest of the creation story, we see that God has a special relationship with the man and woman who have this spirit, Adam and Eve. Yahweh spent time with them, talked with them and taught them. There was a true closeness, intimacy and trust, like a good father would have with his children. God allowed them to share in his creative work by tending the garden and naming the animals. Mankind was innocent in paradise with Yahweh Shalom.

There was nothing between God and his spirit bearers. Perfect peace and harmony, unbroken fellowship. This is how it was supposed to be. This is *normal*. Let's take a moment and enjoy it. Deep breath in . . . and out . . . ahhh. Nice, huh? Unfortunately, we must leave this happy scene because everything is about to become abnormal.

God also has given us something else. It's called a will. With it we make choices. I don't think I need to give you biblical references for this because it's self-evident. We all make choices all the time. Some we would consider good, some of very little consequence, and some bad.

Animals make choices as well but only those that follow their nature. We make choices according to our much deeper knowledge, self-awareness, and our understanding of morality. At least we have ever since Adam and Eve made the first choice to put the pursuit of this knowledge before their relationship with God.

This is where the fall begins. In the Genesis story, God put the tree of the knowledge of good and evil in the garden with them but told them not to eat from it.[2] The tree was not wicked. It was created and placed by a good God. In its fruit was found the morality of God; the higher understanding of what we should and should not do. But God had told them not to eat it.

I have wondered if God had a plan for that tree. Maybe it was there for when Adam and Eve were ready for its knowledge when they had reached a certain level of maturity. Perhaps God was

2. Gen 2:17, NIV.

simply waiting for them to ask about it and he might have given his permission. Only God knows because that's not what happened.

Under the influence of the snake, Eve ate the fruit and Adam followed. But the snake is not the only one to blame. The first couple knew what God had said. God had only one rule and they disobeyed. They rebelled against the God who had given them everything, including their very life. They betrayed the one who had shown them nothing but provision, kindness, and love. They put knowledge before obedience and relationship. Their innocence was at an end.

You may find yourself asking at this point, "Why would God allow Adam and Eve the chance to eat from the tree and gain morality? Didn't it ruin everything?" There was a very important reason. He wanted us to have freedom of moral choice because that is what creates *true love.*

Think about it; can anyone force you to love them? Obviously not. Love must be freely given. Giving us the ability to freely love him was so important to God that he allowed for the consequence. That consequence is being able to choose not to love; to walk away from the author of love.

Therefore, sin entered the world, and everything changed. Their perfect relationship with God was broken and he pronounced judgement on them. Going forward, things would not be so easy. Their fall did not just affect them, it hurt all of creation. They and their descendants would now have to live in a cursed, fallen world. They couldn't stay in the garden because there was another tree there, the tree of life.

> *And the Lord God said, "The man has now become like one of us, knowing good and evil. He must not be allowed to reach out his hand and take also from the tree of life and eat, and live forever." —Gen 3:22*

God would not allow them the opportunity to immortalize their sin and ruin eternity. So, they were banished into the world and *abnormal* became the new normal.

All mankind is now separated from God because of the fall. Our spirit, the place where we meet God, is now left empty. It seems that the longer we are away from true normalcy, the farther mankind falls into this abnormal separation, believing that it is just the way life is; pushing for what our sinful nature wants and ignoring God.

God, however, did not abandon mankind. Years later, he formed a new type of relationship with his chosen people, Israel. It was not the perfect intimate relationship of the garden, but it was worthwhile. He created the Israelites to be set apart as his and gave them his commandments to live by. He watched over them and taught them what it meant to be pure. But because of their sinfulness, they fell short of this standard again and again. God never completely abandoned them because he had a plan. This plan would come out of the heart of the Israelite nation and would eventually bring restoration.

Before I get to that part of the story, we need to get personal. It is easy enough to hear all this and keep it at arm's length, reducing it to an intellectual exercise. But we can't because this is actually a heart exercise and we are intimately involved. We *are* the descendants. Our relationship with God is the one that became broken. Our lives are full of the sin that keeps us separated from God. We are absolutely eyeball deep in it.

Don't believe me? Then allow me to prove it. I'm going to turn the spotlight on you now, so get ready. You need to see yourself through the eyes of a Holy God to understand your sinfulness. Why? Because sin has become so commonplace that we don't even realize how much we do it. To facilitate this, I will use God's law, the ten commandments.

You can find them in Exodus chapter 20. Read through all ten, and as you do, consider how each one affects relationships. Apart from perhaps number four, it is clear they all address something that would harm a relationship if broken or help a relationship if followed. Not surprisingly, God is all about keeping and mending relationships. I could pick any commandment for my examples, but it is easy enough to start with number one.

You shall have no other gods before me. —Exod 20:3

Consider for a moment what you are running after in life. What motivates you? What do you find yourself thinking about? What do you spend your time, energy, and resources on? What influences most of your decisions? Take a moment before you continue reading and contemplate this.

By now, you probably have an answer and I bet it is not God. Is it money? Sex? Success? Thrills? Comfort? There are lots of forms of good old-fashioned selfishness.

Perhaps it is something you would consider good, such as knowledge or work. However, whatever that thing is, God's law states that it is an idol if it comes before him. You have made it into a little god and placed it in front of God in your life. God deserves to be the center of your world, but you marginalize or even completely ignore him. That just shows the brokenness of your relationship with him. Not a good start.

How about commandment number three?

> *You shall not misuse the name of the Lord your God, for the Lord will not hold anyone guiltless who misuses his name. —Exod 20:7*

Would you agree that using his name as a curse word, in disgust or anger would qualify as as misuse? Yet it happens all the time. Take a look at your phone texts. How many OMGs, GDs and JCs show up? How often do they pop out of your mouth when you are excited, mad, frustrated, or just spicing up the conversation? Are these said out of reverence and love? It's not just that it is wrong and irreverent, but it is done without any thought or consideration for the one whom you are naming. Strike two.

Shall we move on? Commandment number eight should be easy enough.

> *You shall not steal. —Exod 20:15*

That is crystal clear. Don't take stuff that belongs to someone else. Perhaps you have never robbed a bank. Good for you. But the commandment does not say "don't steal big stuff," it says don't steal. That means the candy that was in your classmate's backpack or the parking space that was reserved. It also does not need to be material things like fruit from the produce section or office supplies. Stealing is taking anything that does not belong to you. It can be ideas, time, attention, hearts, or reputations. As you consider this expanded definition, you know you are not innocent. No one likes to be called a thief but if the moniker fits, wear it.

Okay, for the sake of your dignity, I will only do one more: commandment number nine.

> *You shall not give false testimony against your neighbor.*
> *—Exod 20:16*

Perhaps the best way to describe this commandment is lying in a way that hurts someone else. We generally do this to protect ourselves. When you deflect blame onto another, you give false testimony. It happens at home when you throw your sibling under the bus when you were involved in the naughtiness as well. It happens in the workplace when you want the boss to be angrier at your co-worker than you. It happens when you are mad at your spouse and decide to embellish the story of how they wronged you. It happens in court when winning your case is more important than telling the truth. In other words, it happens.

So basically, I have just called you an idolatrous, lying, thieving, blasphemer. And that was just four of the ten commandments. You can be angry at me if you want but you need to face up to the truth. If you think you are a good person, God's law shows differently.

You are a sinner. It comes out in your selfishness, in your judgmental attitude, in your antagonistic anger, in your push to be in the front of the line, in your mean thoughts that sometimes slip out, in your impatience with others, in your dark moods, in your unforgiveness, in your passive-aggressiveness, in your vanity, and in your lack of thoughtfulness.

In fact, I am certain of something about you. I will show you by becoming a mind reader. Actually, the term *heart* reader works better. I am certain that as you consider this idea of sin in your life that something specific comes to mind. Some immoral event, recurring inappropriate appetite or attitude that you are ashamed of. Something that you wouldn't want others to know about. Some hidden secret that you hope never comes out. Am I right? Whatever it is, it's an example of your sinfulness.

If you were gut-level honest, you would admit that not only do you sin, but you often relish it. I know that I did. It often feels good in the moment to do bad things. The amusement of making fun of someone else. The danger of walking on the dark side. The thrill of a sexual tryst.

But humanity has gone a step further. Our world finds ways to celebrate sin. Our gluttony becomes all-you-can-eat buffets where more food is wasted than eaten. Our greed becomes gaudy jewelry, fancy cars, and huge homes while others go without. Our lustfulness is glorified in movies and is proclaimed "the sexual revolution." We admire and envy Hollywood stars whom we *literally* call idols and we can't wait to find out what these fallen people are doing next. Yes, our sin goes very deep and it has cursed the world.

I hope you are saying, "Wow, that really hurts, but there is more truth in there than I want to admit." Well, you need to admit it. Only then will you begin to see yourself rightly instead of through rose-colored glasses. We have already learned that we are made in God's image. That's the good part. But we are also sinful through and through. Adam and Eve may have started this mess for mankind, but we choose to leave our relationship with a Holy God broken and wallow in our sinfulness.

Why am I harping on this and making you want to throw this book against the wall? Because, if you do not realize you are a sinner, you will not realize your need for a savior. If you do not realize your need of a savior, you are not going to let him fix your relationship with God. The deeper you realize your sin goes, the more actively you will seek out his help.

If it makes you feel any better, we are all in the same boat. Romans 3:23 states:

> *. . . for all have sinned and fall short of the glory of God . . .*

But that boat is sinking. Normal is fading and abnormal is firmly in control. We desperately need Jesus to make things right because we can't fix it ourselves. Let me show you what I mean.

The Fix

Often, when I get into a spiritual conversation with someone, I will ask a pointed question. It is designed to help clarify a fundamental aspect of being human. The question is, "are you basically a dependent or independent creature?" Before you read any further, consider that question for a moment. What do you think? Are you reliant on other things and people or not?

Most people will answer with something like, "I'm an adult. I got through school and no longer live with my parents. I think for myself and support myself financially. Therefore, I am independent." OK, but look a little deeper.

Beneath a veneer of independence, we are actually profoundly dependent. Think of all the things we need to live—air, water, food, shelter, light, warmth, clothing, companionship, medicine. Without any one of these things, our lives would be severely crippled or over. Our modern lifestyle takes this further. Today, we need electricity, plumbing, garbage collection, A/C, cars, refrigerators, batteries, computers, and other gadgets galore. We like to think we control them but don't be fooled. Consider what happens when the electricity goes out. Our world comes to a standstill!

Why bring this up? Because we are ultimately dependent on our creator without whom we would have nothing. He gave us our brain to think with, our body to navigate this world with, and our spirit to go beyond. God created us dependent because this condition encourages relationship just as independence can make us move away from relationship. When we realize we cannot do it all by ourselves, we seek out help and companionship. In the end, this should lead us back to God.

I can't help but think about atheists when I consider this. Of course, they are dependent creatures right along with us. However, without accepting God, they can only be dependent on the lifeless, mindless, heartless laws of the universe that they believe happened by chance. That can't be very encouraging. I wonder if it ever keeps them up at night.

This brings us to the third theme of the Bible, redemption. In considering how our relationship with God is fixed, many of us think it is something we do. But in this, we are also dependent on God. The most common misconception is that we can live our lives in a way whereby our good deeds outweigh our bad. We think we can simply make up for our bad deeds by doing more good deeds. If we can't reach holy, we can at least try to reach good enough. Then, God is required to let us into Heaven and back in his good graces, right? Let's look at why this is not true.

Consider this example. A man steals a car. He is not caught for his theft, but over time he ends up feeling guilty. He becomes a law-abiding citizen and even gives money to charities to try and make up for his crime. Having done these good things, is the man no longer a thief? Is it as if he never committed the crime in the first place? Of course not. He is still guilty of a crime. If the law caught up to him, he would rightly be convicted. So it is with our sins.

This belief that good deeds make up for our sins is so prevalent I would like to belabor the point for a moment by telling you a fable.

There once was a king who hated taking baths. Since he was king, no one could force him to take one. So, the king didn't wash himself and became quite smelly. His abundant body odor could be sniffed from a great distance. Everyone in his court became distressed because they often had to be in the company of the king for long periods of time.

It finally got so bad that his most trusted advisor worked up the nerve to confront him about it. He begged the king to do something about his foul smell. To his credit, the king listened and understood the concern of the court. But he still did not want to bathe. So, he came up with the idea to try and cover up his body odor with perfumes.

Pleased with his solution, he walked into court the next day with copious amounts applied. But the effect was anything but pleasant. The courtiers were now forced to deal with the smell of eye-watering sweetness with an aftershock of pungent nastiness that only served to turn their stomachs all the more.

I hope the moral of this story is obvious. We cannot cover up our foul-smelling sins with the perfume of good works. We need a bath.

Perhaps you are proud of the many good things you have done in your life. Congratulations. But all your sin is still there and must be accounted for. Not to mention the fact that God should ultimately get the credit for our good deeds. The Bible says:

> *Every good and perfect gift is from above, coming down from the Father of the heavenly lights . . . —Jas 1:17*

You were made in the image of God. If you can do good things, thank God.

To be perfectly just, God *must* condemn every sin. No exceptions. Remember, Heaven will be completely swept clean of all evil. He would not allow Adam and Eve the chance to stay in the garden and immortalize their sin, and the same goes for us. You now know that you have a multitude of sins. Just like in a court of law, the penalty for that sin must be paid. If you have done the crime, you're going to do the time. Unless of course, someone else pays your penalty for you.

Enter Jesus Christ.

God knew the predicament fashioned by the gift of choice that allowed for true love. He knew that we would all fall into sin and He knew that sin must be condemned. He knew we could not make up for it ourselves. So, his plan included a solution, and that solution was a beautifully personal way to fix our relationship with him. Of course it was; he is our relational God.

The solution did not come in the form of some special knowledge to solve the riddle of life. It did not come in the form of a magical incantation or elaborate ceremony. It did not come in the form of a mysterious relic or a holy mountain to climb. It came in the form of a person. A person who was willing to make a sacrifice. The sacrifice that paid for all sin.

The story is told in the four biblical Gospels that God came into the world in the person of Jesus. In his flesh, he was fully human, but he did not commit any sin. He perfectly followed his father's will and spread truth, love, and healing everywhere he went. He showed through the scriptures that it had been foretold that the Messiah, the king who would be our savior, would come. He announced that he was that Messiah and proved it through many miracles.

During his time on earth, he healed the sick, calmed the waters, fed the multitudes, and even raised people from the dead. He turned water into wine, filled nets with fish, and revealed his true self by being transfigured in front of his disciples, becoming radiant in glory upon a mountain top. His words were truth, his deeds were wondrous, his wisdom was bottomless, and his heart was golden. He was the only one who could be worthy to make the ultimate sacrifice.

He foretold of his own death and resurrection, then walked the path of sorrows. He was betrayed by a friend and falsely accused by the religious authorities. He was brought before the Roman Governor and though innocent, condemned. He was beaten and mocked and made to carry his own cross to the place of death where he was nailed to it. Even as he hung there dying, he said:

> *"Father, forgive them, for they do not know what they are doing." —Luke 23:34*

His heart was unwavering in his mission of forgiveness and cleansing. He went through it all so that you would not have to die in your sins and face condemnation. He did it to wash you, to redeem you. With his final breath, he said:

> *"It is finished." —John 19:30*

The sacrifice had been made and his mission was complete. The door to our relationship with God was about to be opened. In some miraculous symbolism, the curtain that covered the entrance of the most holy place in the Jewish temple was ripped in half from top to bottom. This room was where God had told the Israelites his presence would dwell. The veil which had separated God and man had been torn asunder. The spiritual was made available to those in the material. There was now hope that our spirits could be refilled with God's presence; that normal could return.

If this were all that happened, what Jesus had accomplished would have remained unproven. But, to show that Jesus had power over sin and death, more was to come. They placed his body in a tomb and rolled a stone over the entrance. Three days passed. The tomb was found open. The stone had been rolled away and Jesus was gone. Angels told the disciples that Jesus had not been taken, he had been brought back to life!

Perhaps right here you are having a hard time with this story. People don't come back to life. Not after being dead for three days. It is a bit much to swallow. Isn't there a simple explanation? This is just too miraculous.

You're right. It is impossible for this to have happened . . . without Yahweh. It is either a farce or it was done by an all-powerful God.

Think back on what we have learned. This universe could never have come into being by chance; something does not come from nothing. But here it is. It should not be orderly in a way that gives us a purposeful reality. Yet it does. Never has life come from non-life. But we are on a planet full of it. There is no reason for life to be so intensely relational. But interconnections are everywhere we look. We have no idea how we came to be so different from the animals. Yet, we are deeply intelligent, moral creatures.

When you bring the glow-in-the-dark God to the foreground, of course this can happen. The creator of the universe can operate his creation as he wishes. The author of life has control over death. The Father can easily bring life back into the Son. And he did.

The Gospels proclaim that Jesus came back to the disciples alive and well and showed himself to hundreds of people. In the end, he was taken up into Heaven. Jesus went back home, but because of the reality of the spiritual, he also remained with his disciples. Jesus' resurrection showed that he had truly conquered sin and death. He wants *you* to take advantage of that fact.

Let's assume for a moment that you want the salvation provided by Jesus and you want to be connected to God. You no longer want sin to pervade your life and abnormal to be your normal. How exactly does one go about it? As I said in the last chapter, it is a heart issue.

When I say heart issue, I do not mean warm and fuzzy emotions. You may end up with some by the end, but I mean something deeper. It is about ideals such as love, peace, hope, goodness, faith, freedom, and truth. Your brain can understand them, but they are *expressed* at a heart level. These values are in your heart because they were put there to prompt you toward our creator, the God of all good things.

Once we understand this, we begin by looking at what God has to say.

> *Yet to all who did receive him, to those who believed in his name, he gave the right to become children of God—children born not of natural descent, nor of human decision or a husband's will, but born of God. —John 1:12–13*

Let's break this verse down. First it says, "*yet to all who did receive him.*" This is the relational heart of the good news, or gospel, presented in the Bible. That is all that is required; just receive him. But we should consider *how* to receive him. We are to humbly, honestly, and whole-heartedly receive Jesus into our life.

When I say "humbly," I want you to recall the principle we discovered earlier: Want to see him? Call on him. Don't want to see him? Don't call on him. While this is true, I also noted that the Bible says more to illuminate this. Here is that clarification:

> *God opposes the proud but shows favor to the humble.*
> *—Jas 4:6*

In other words, God has no intention of responding to the call of someone who pursues him pridefully. You have nothing to offer but a humble heart in receiving Jesus.

When I say "honestly," I mean you are not going to fool God.

> *God, who knows the heart, showed that he accepted them by giving the Holy Spirit . . . —Acts 15:8*

He knows your intentions. He sees through any false motives. You must honestly want Jesus.

When I say "whole-heartedly," I mean Jesus cannot be partially received. Being half-hearted in this does not cut it and it is greatly disrespectful to the one who made the sacrifice. You cannot go to Jesus in a wishy-washy way still harboring sin. The Bible has many verses about repentance of sins, such as:

> *. . . Jesus began to preach, "Repent, for the kingdom of heaven has come near." —Matt 4:17*

To repent means that your attitude towards your sin changes. No more relishing and celebrating sin. No more wallowing in some form of immorality. You turn from how you once saw your sin and agree with God that it is wrong. To put it in modern vernacular, you have to unfriend your sin.

If seen in the light of God's holiness, sin is repulsive. "Repulsive" is actually a great descriptor for sin. When seen properly, it should literally repulse you away from sinfulness and into God's loving arms. Your attitude toward sin must change because you cannot both hold your sins dear and ask Jesus to cleanse you of them. This is an exchange; you give Christ your sins and he gives you his righteousness.[1] What an incredible deal!

To look at it in relational terms, at the moment of salvation your allegiance changes from your sinfulness to God. For example, the traditional wedding vows generally have a phrase that goes "forsaking all others, I give myself to you." Your new spouse would expect nothing less. Do you think our holy God would allow you to continue to love your sin and come into relationship with him?

1. 2 Cor 5:21, NIV.

God understands that no one is perfect. We all fail, and there is grace for that. But our hearts now become attuned to him and the sin that kept us from him no longer has favor.

The next part of the verse says, "*to those who believed in his name.*" We have already seen that one descriptive name for Jesus is Immanuel; God with us. He is given many names in scripture including Savior, Lord, Son of God, and Light of the World. To believe in his name is to believe these truths about him.

This is not just intellectual consent. It is not enough to simply accept that there was a person named Jesus. What it fully means is to place your faith in him; to trust him, who he is, and what he did.

> *Trust in the Lord with all your heart and lean not on your own understanding . . . —Prov 3:5*

We all know that trust is the absolute bedrock of a strong relationship. To trust Jesus is to choose to put your life into his hands. This means that you are taking your life *out* of your own hands. It is admitting that he should be utmost, and you should follow him.

First, you trust him to fix your relationship with God and then you faithfully *relate* with him. You bring him into every aspect of your life and walk with him through it. You can do this because he will literally come and set up residency within you in the person of the Holy Spirit. Remember when we talked about indwelling? This is it. From the day of your salvation forward, Jesus is with you.

There is one other detail that I need to make clear about this. Some people ask, "Is believing in Jesus the only way to be saved?" Absolutely. Why? Because he is the only one who has made the sacrifice. No one else has. We cannot make the sacrifice; we can only receive the sacrifice from the Savior.

The last part of the verse says, "*. . . he gave the right to become children of God.*" I have already discussed how it is appropriate to call people children of God because he is our creator. Perhaps you remember me telling you that, at salvation, this takes on a much deeper meaning. This verse says Jesus gives us a special new right.

At the moment of salvation, we are no longer simply a creation of God. We become much more. Jesus expounds on this later when he says:

> *Very truly I tell you, no one can see the kingdom of God unless they are born again. —John 3:3*

The idea of rebirth expressed in this verse is completely appropriate. It is a new beginning, a quickening of the spirit. It is a birth *into* a family. We are now a part of the spiritual family of God!

It is no accident that the family is the basic unit that God uses for human relationship. You have a unique, one of a kind kinship to your birth parents. There is only one union that created you. Your genealogy is made up half by your father and half by your mother. If you have siblings, those relationships are singular as well. No one else could be your biological brother or sister except those born of your parents.

Families in a fallen world can be more complicated and messy, but God's intentions are to give us a safe, loving place where we grow up and where we always know we belong. The ideal is that your family is always your family. It is what makes up the basis of your identity.

Your new spiritual family is the perfect manifestation of this. You are given a new identity in Christ and God becomes your father in the most complete sense of the word. You may have been short-changed in the area of family in this world. If you were, I am truly sorry this happened to you. It can be very painful to be in a broken family.

But that is why this news is so wonderful, because it is different with God. His family is unblemished and eternal. You will always be safe. You will always be loved. You will always have a home. You will always be his child. You will always belong. I told you his plan is immensely relational, and it is.

This entire process is made possible by grace, the most wonderfully relational thing that can be imagined! Grace is God's unmerited love. Because God loves you; because God *is* love, he is willing to forgive you and give you his grace. Christ's sacrifice is payment in full on your behalf.

> *For the wages of sin is death, but the gift of God is eternal life in Christ Jesus our Lord. —Rom 6:23*

God gives it as a gracious *gift* to us. All we need to do is receive it with the right heart. The result is a right relationship with God and that relationship is eternal.

Forever

ONE OF THE THINGS I enjoy doing is watching videos about old things being restored. I become engrossed watching new life being breathed into a vintage muscle car or wood from an old barn being used to create a beautiful dining room table under the hand of a master craftsman. There is something deeply satisfying about seeing an item that was going to waste; something that was broken, rusting away, and destined for the scrap heap being revitalized. The rust flying off the metal as the rotating wire brush makes it gleam again. The sanding of the boards to bring out the heart of the wood. The dull blade being honed to a razor-sharp edge. The reconditioning oil being rubbed into the leather. The buffing of the surface to a glossy new shine.

Rarely is the goal of the restoration to simply bring something back to its original condition. Most of the time, the article ends up being better; a unique, one of a kind design that is as much a piece of art as it is a utilitarian item. Perhaps part of the reason this is satisfying is that we share God's creative passions. Not only do we enjoy creating but *re*creating as well.

It also plays into our sense of fairness. Everything and everyone deserve a second chance. No one wants to feel as if they have been thrown on the scrap heap of life after they have messed up. Surely, we still have value after we have been scarred and broken—even if many of those scars are from self-inflicted wounds. Lucky for all of us, God sees it the same way.

Although it is nice to see something restored, satisfaction in this world is slippery. The things we enjoy all seem to fall short of real fulfillment. Sure, something might be enjoyable for a while, but everything tends to lose its luster. We always end up looking for another project to dig into, a new thrill to chase, a different mountain to climb, another trophy to win.

There is a reason for this. We were never meant to find perfect fulfillment in this material world. Somewhere deep within ourselves, we realize the truth that this is all temporary. It is not built to last forever. We have one mortal lifetime and it certainly does not feel like enough.

The image of God within us whispers that there is something more. Something that will be deeply satisfying. Something that will give us our true purpose. Something that will restore everything and make it shiny new; even better than the original. Something that is not temporary.

The final theme in the Bible is restoration. Although the act of restoration begins with salvation, the Bible promises us a day when all things will be made right.

> *He who was seated on the throne said, "I am making everything new!" —Rev 21:5*

This last theme is more difficult to discuss because most of the restoration is yet to come. If you have received Christ, your spirit is renewed but you are still in the fallen world. The promise of God is that it will not stay this way. He is going to restore his creation. We will not simply go back to the Garden of Eden. God is doing something greater than that.

Salvation opens the door for us, but restoration is God and all things good and spiritual moving in. It will happen at the end of time when God is completing what he has planned for the universe. The veil I spoke of earlier between the material and the spiritual will be removed completely. God's restoration will bring radical change.

No one can be sure exactly what this process will be like. God might just start over and completely erase the material universe in favor of the spiritual. But I know that God is big on restoration and renewal. He renews each person that receives Christ rather than doing away with them and starting from scratch.

So, I can't help but think that he will do the same with the rest of creation. I believe the material will be dramatically improved by being *infused* with the spiritual. That was the way God had always intended for it to be. All the sin, death, and evil will be scrubbed away, and the spiritual infusion will bring new life to everything in a spectacular way!

Today, we are still in the times of redemption and can only see a glimpse of the restoration. The book of Revelation gives us some idea about it, but so much of that book is still cloaked in prophesy about the future. Because we still live in a mortal, fallen, material world, the restoration can be difficult to imagine. A world that is a mix of good and bad is all we have ever known. Time ticking away and everything growing old. The cycle of life and death going on, season after season, is the rule. So it is hard to wrap our heads around a perfectly good and eternal spiritual creation.

Maybe I'm weird, but I often think about this. I have read and re-read the last chapters of Revelation again and again, soaking in it and looking for new clues. As we saw earlier, these chapters are a description of the restoration and Heaven itself. What will it be like when Heaven comes down to Earth? How will we spend our time when we have nothing but time going on forever? It can take some effort and imagination, but a picture can begin to come into view. And it is stunningly beautiful.

These days most computers have stock photos that can be used as screen savers. These pictures are often perfectly photoshopped shots of ideal natural areas. Things such as pristine tropical beaches, mossy stones peeking out of gurgling brooks, deer grazing in green meadows with soft sunlight filtering through tree branches. I find myself longing to be there in the serenity and beauty of it all.

But how gorgeous would these scenes be if it were infused with the spirit? Like shimmering, miraculous pixie dust making everything more alive, more animated, more *real* than it has ever been. How amazing would our world be if this was the way everything looked no matter where you laid your eyes?

That is a nice place to start, but the effect of the restoration on nature goes well beyond this. In the book of Isaiah, we see some imagery that might be giving us a glimpse.

> *The wolf will live with the lamb, the leopard will lie down with the goat, the calf and the lion and the yearling together; and a little child will lead them. The cow will feed with the bear, their young will lie down together, and the lion will eat straw like the ox. The infant will play near the cobra's den, and the young child will put its hand into the viper's nest. They will neither harm nor destroy . . .*
> *—Isa 11:6–9*

In other words, survival of the fittest will no longer be needed because death is done away with after the restoration. There will be no predation nor prey. This also means no thorns on the bushes, no insects will sting or bite, no need to fear going into the water. Nature will be perfectly safe, and the animals will have no fear. We will not be separate from nature; we will commune beautifully with it.

In Revelation chapter 21, the Apostle John gives us a wonderful description of the city of God, the New Jerusalem, coming down as the heavenly spiritual invades the material after the judgement. Although his attempts to describe it fall short because he only has material words, he describes a gleaming beauty filled with all things truly valuable. The entire city glistens with the brilliance of a precious stone. It appears to be made of glassy gold and the foundations are encrusted with a dozen kinds of jewels. The city walls look like jasper and the twelve gates are huge pearls.

The city is massive and described as being a perfect cube in dimensions. If we understand the measurements correctly, the base of the city would not be able to fit within the north and south borders of the continental United States. Because it is a cube, it is as tall as it is wide, so there will be plenty of room!

But the natural world and the city are just the setting. They are simply the place where we will be as we enjoy God and each other for eternity. This is where it gets truly exciting because we get to imagine a world without sin and death hindering our lives. To do this, we need to have some understanding of what sin does and how its absence will benefit us.

Sin separates. In fact, I would say that is its main function. The sin of disobedience separated Adam and Eve from God. The sin of adultery separates a man and his wife. The sin of greed separates two business partners. The sin of envy separates the one with little from the one with plenty. The sin of theft separates a person from their possessions. The sin of discord unravels a relationship while the sin of unforgiveness keeps it broken.

Sin separates relationships because, almost without exception, sin is a selfish thing. So many times, it is putting yourself before someone else. Of course, this puts a strain on a relationship. A girl's jealousy of her sister's beauty makes her grow cold toward her sibling. A worker's want for the promotion makes him harbor ill-will toward a rival workmate. When two men vie for the attention of the same woman, the other man is the bad guy.

The separating effect of sin is easily seen in things such as racism where people or groups different than us are hated simply because they are an easy target upon which to displace our anger. But most of the time it is more personal. We judge others' actions harshly while giving ourselves every excuse. We assume bad intentions without talking to the other person. We build a tall fence around our property and don't bother to get to know our neighbors. We isolate because interacting with others can be draining. We don't make an effort to tell our spouse why we love them.

We all do it. Our sins separate us. In a thousand different ways, our relationships are in danger from sin every day. But what if there were no sin? What would begin to happen? How would our relationships heal? No misunderstandings, no bad intentions, no hurt feelings. No jealousy, envy or distrust. No false motives, hidden agendas, lying, or masks. No reason to protect our feelings because everyone is trustworthy. No defensive walls shooting up because no one is pushing our buttons. Every misstep restored by instant forgiveness. What if there were no longer sin in the way of any relationship; neither your sin nor theirs?

Imagine the best, most intimate evening that you have ever had with close friends and family. There was probably a lovely meal and something to celebrate. Everyone got along and enjoyed the company of everyone else. Remember the sharing, caring, laughter, familiarity, understanding, connections, and warm feelings? Remember how no one wanted the evening to end and there were hugs and tears as you went your separate ways?

This is how it will be in Heaven between everyone all the time. *All* the time. No sin to interrupt. You will be swimming in the warm wishes, kindness, acceptance, peace, and good-will of your spiritual family. The family you were created to be in.

To top this off, you will be in the presence of your true father. His love and strength will radiate throughout your existence, a constant reminder of who you are to him; his beloved child. He will give you your true name and true purpose and you will be deeply satisfied fulfilling that purpose.

> *No longer will there be any curse. The throne of God and of the Lamb will be in the city, and his servants will serve him. They will see his face, and his name will be on their foreheads. There will be no more nights. They will not need the light of a lamp or the light of the sun, for the Lord God will give them light. And they will reign for ever and ever.*
> *—Rev 22:3–5*

We will see the face of God. We will be surrounded by his presence. He will be our light and we will never experience darkness again. This is the end game. This is what God planned all along. He will be with us in intimate, uninterrupted communion.

The best part will be that it will never end. When Jesus spoke of the promise of salvation, he always called it "*eternal* life." He said it again and again. In his resurrection, Christ defeated death right along with sin. In fact, Revelation describes death being permanently ended during the judgement pronounced in chapter 20.

In Heaven, there will never be a time when you go your separate ways nor a time when you will never see someone again.

Everyone will always be there enjoying this new reality with God forever. For all eternity. Without the chains of sin and death, what heights will we obtain? It is hard to imagine, but it is heart-warming to try.

I hope this vision of God's ultimate kingdom has allowed you to shake off your mortality for a moment and see why his offer of eternal life is so wondrous and important. If you are anything like me, your heart longs for such things. That longing is a signpost put there by God saying, "Come, my child, and enjoy all that I have in store for you." All you need to do is take his hand.

Conclusion

THANK YOU SO MUCH for taking this journey with me. My hope was to give you a fresh perspective on God. I wanted to make him tangible to you, not just a vague concept or a distant figure in an ancient book. He is real and imminent, and he wants you to know him.

Since becoming a Christian, I have listened to hundreds of sermons. Many of them were outstanding and helped me understand different aspects of God and my faith. But I learned one of the more essential theological concepts from an interesting source while nowhere near a church.

As many of my readers may know, during the nineteen seventies and eighties, there was a hit TV show called M*A*S*H; a comedy series set during the Korean war detailing the misadventures of doctors and nurses in a mobile hospital unit. With iconic characters such as Hawkeye, Klinger, and Radar, the show kept the laughs coming in stark contrast to the absurdities of the war happening all around them. With the humor, there were also many poignant moments exploring different aspects of being human in a trying situation.

While watching reruns of M*A*S*H, I saw one such moment in an episode in which Father Mulcahy, the unit's chaplain, gave a moving sermon. In most of the episodes, Father Mulcahy was simply there to be a foil to all the misconduct going on at the camp. However, in this sermon he said something profound: "God . . .

created us so he could be here himself; so that he could exist in the lives of those he created in his image."[1]

This is a beautiful assertion. God created us to *relate* with him. That was one of God's central reasons for giving us life and making us in his image. So, based on this assertion, I want to leave my readers with a couple of questions.

First, to those of you who have not placed your faith in Christ; what's stopping you? If you still have honest questions, seek out the answers. Don't let this be an, "I'll look into it someday," situation. It is too important to put on the back burner.

I came to Christ as an adult in my late twenties and regret all the time I wasted running from God. All I did during that time was hand my life over to sinfulness and make it into a mess. Getting into right relationship with God is the start of living your life for the reason you were created. There is nothing more satisfying than that.

There is nothing more important we can do with our lives; no higher purpose, no greater good. Your union with God can bring you peace, joy, hope, love, and a sense of security that can be found nowhere else. Your life will become an adventure as you follow him, reverberating with real maturation, challenges worth tackling, and a purpose of eternal significance. There is nothing boring about truly living as a child of God and that relationship goes on forever.

Second, to those of you who have received Christ; do you see your faith this way? Do you think of it as a relationship? Do you take Proverbs 3:6 literally, acknowledging him in every aspect of your life and cultivating the relationship you have with him? Do you communicate often with him, spend time with him, bring him into your decisions, and invite him to be with you as you live out your life?

The greatest gift God could give us is himself. He loves us deeply and he wants us to fall in love with him. He doesn't put restrictions on when or how often we come to him, he simply wants us to come. With this relationality in mind, open yourself to new

1. Morgan, *M*A*S*H*.

depths of adulation, dedication and communion you've shied from or never considered. If you do this, it will absolutely revolutionize and invigorate your faith walk. This is the way our faith was meant to be with our relational God!

Bibliography

Bernock, Daniel. "What Does it Mean That God is Our Abba Father?" Christianity.com, June 22, 2020. https://www.christianity.com/wiki/god/what-does-it-mean-that-god-is-our-abba-father.html.

Bible Project. "God." bibleproject.com/explore/god/.

Bowyer, Jerry. "God In Mathematics." *Forbes*, April 21, 2016. www.forbes.com/sites/jerrybowyer/2016/04/19/where-does-math-come-from-a-mathematiciantheologian-talks-about-the-limits-of-numbers/#346aca564a3a.

Christian Research. "The Bible." Christianresearch.org. www.christian-research.org/reports/archives-and-statistics/the-bible/.

Dictionary.com. "Survival of the Fittest." www.dictionary.com/browse/survival-of-the-fittest.

Ellis, Ian. "Geometry and Experience." Einstein—Geometry and Experience, todayinsci.com/E/Einstein_Albert/Einstein-GeometryAndExperience.htm.

Gilbert, Josiah H. "Clarke, James Freeman." In *Dictionary of Burning Words of Brilliant Writers*, edited by Josiah H. Gilbert, 563. New York: Ketcham, 1895.

Institute for Creation Research. "Earth Was Created in a Wonderful Location," Icr.org, www.icr.org/earths-location

Kalu, Madeline. "What Does it Mean That God is Jehova-Rapha?" Christianity.com, www.christianity.com/wiki/god/what-does-it-mean-that-god-is-jehova-rapha.html.

Kalu, Madeline. "What Is the Meaning of Shekinah Glory?" Christianity.com, www.christianity.com/wiki/christian-terms/what-is-the-meaning-of-shekinah-glory.html.

Morgan, Harry, dir. *M*A*S*H*. Season 9, episode 18, "Blood Brothers." Aired April 6, 1981, on CBS. https://www.hulu.com/series/ae94231d-0f04-482a-b9ee-9911e339e3ed.

NASA Science. "Black Holes," Science.nasa.gov, www.science.nasa.gov/astrophysics/focus-areas/black-holes

National Geographic. "Fire Ants Make Living Raft." Nationalgeographic.com. https://video.nationalgeographic.com/video/00000144–0a33-d3cb-a96c-7b3feaa10000.

Parsons, John J. "The Hebrew Names for God—El." Hebrew for Christians. www.hebrew4christians.com/Names_of_G-d/El/el.html.

Piper, Barnabas. "Jehovah Jireh Meaning: 'The Lord Will Provide.'" Bible Study Tools. www.biblestudytools.com/bible-study/topical-studies/jehovah-jireh-the-lord-will-provide.html.

Poythress, Vern S. *Redeeming Mathematics: a God-Centered Approach.* Wheaton, IL: Crossway, 2015.

Rees, Martin J. *Just Six Numbers: The Deep Forces That Shape the Universe.* London: Phoenix Mass Market, 2003.

Ryan, Joel. "What Does it Mean That God is Jehovah-Shalom?" Christianity.com, July 17, 2019. www.christianity.com/wiki/god/what-does-it-mean-that-god-is-jehovah-shalom.html.

Sagan, Carl. *Pale Blue Dot: A Vision of the Human Future in Space.* New York: Ballantine, 1994.

Science Digest, Volume 89, 1981. The University of Michigan.

Schultz, Carl. "Spirit Definition and Meaning—Bible Dictionary." Bible Study Tools. www.biblestudytools.com/dictionary/spirit/.

Seybold, Matt. "The Apocryphal Twain: 'The two most important days of your life . . . '" Center for Mark Twain Studies, December 6, 2016. www.marktwainstudies.com/the-apocryphal-twain-the-two-most-important-days-of-your-life/.

Sustainable Human. "How Wolves Change Rivers," *YouTube*, February 13, 2014. https://www.youtube.com/watch?v=ysa5OBhXz-Q.

Team Africa Geographic. "Understanding Lion Infanticide," Africa Geographic. www.africageographic.com/stories/understanding-lion-infanticide. TedGlobalLondon. "Everything you think you know about addiction is wrong," Johann Hari, June 2015, www.ted.com/talks/johann_hari_everything_you_think_you_know_about_addiction_is_wrong.

Zalasiewicz, Jan, and Mark Williams. *The Goldilocks Planet: The Four Billion Year Story of Earth's Climate.* Oxford: Oxford University Press, 2012.

CPSIA information can be obtained
at www.ICGtesting.com
Printed in the USA
FSHW020831220321
79623FS